GUIDEBOOK FOR SUPPORTING DECISION MAKING UNDER UNCERTAINTIES

Today's Managers, Tomorrow's Business

GUIDEBOOK FOR SUPPORTING DECISION MAKING UNDER UNCERTAINTIES

Today's Managers, Tomorrow's Business

Ettore Piccirillo

Massimo G Noro

 **World Scientific**

NEW JERSEY · LONDON · SINGAPORE · BEIJING · SHANGHAI · HONG KONG · TAIPEI · CHENNAI

Published by

World Scientific Publishing Co. Pte. Ltd.

5 Toh Tuck Link, Singapore 596224

USA office: 27 Warren Street, Suite 401-402, Hackensack, NJ 07601

UK office: 57 Shelton Street, Covent Garden, London WC2H 9HE

British Library Cataloguing-in-Publication Data
A catalogue record for this book is available from the British Library.

GUIDEBOOK FOR SUPPORTING DECISION MAKING UNDER UNCERTAINTIES
Today's Managers, Tomorrow's Business

ISBN-13 978-981-270-803-8
ISBN-10 981-270-803-0

Typeset by Stallion Press
Email: enquiries@stallionpress.com

Printed in Singapore.

CONTENTS

PROLOGUE

How did we actually get started? Let us be honest. The genesis of this work was quite fortuitous, and the first ideas have been bounced around over lunch, and in a foreign language! Three of us, all of Italian origin, used to get together for lunch and complain about the British weather, the NHS health system, and the awful pizzas served at the local restaurant.

But then, we would elevate the level of the philosophical discussion on what is really needed to make a sound business decision. As a matter of fact, we are a diverse group of researchers with different backgrounds and on different career paths. But what can you expect when you put an economist, a physicist, and an information scientist together? The diverse and complementary knowledge that each one of us brought to the table enables cross fertilisation of ideas, a different way of framing the problem, and an alternative vocabulary to describe how to formulate the solution.

Our complementary interests, and frames of mind came together to make new connections, to generate new ideas and to close the circle of creative solutions.

This idea became a working hypothesis, then a Friday afternoon reading activity, then a chartered R&D project, and finally it was completed and refined through a valuable collaboration with Cambridge University. The output of our work has been presented to several international conferences, and was always well received by the financial and the supply chain/logistics community.

Our proposal has appealed to more than one 'Business Consultant'. This is why we have decided to put it all down on paper, and write this book...

The objective of this work is to provide guidance to the business leader or decision maker, in order to make sound business decisions. This analysis will appeal to investment appraisal practitioners, such as strategic planners, business analysts, financial partners and supply chain experts alike. By supply chain, here we mean the network of retailers, distributors, transporters, storage facilities and suppliers that participate in the sale, delivery and production of a particular product.

Taking into account the complexity and specificity of the matter in discussion, the work starts with an introduction of the concept of decision making under uncertainty, and the forces driving the business. A gap in the current knowledge is then exposed as it arises from an analysis of the profitability indicators now in use. With deep hands-on decision making within the supply chain environment, and coupling with leading edge mathematical and business formulations, we propose how to enrich quantitative and qualitative decision making measures. This leads naturally into a decision making framework and process, supported by a ready-to-use tool (PADOVA).

ACKNOWLEDGEMENTS

This book is the result of a long project, and we must give credit to several people whose work was central to steering this journey in the right direction.

Dr Filippo Neri started this journey with us, and without his witty questions this work would have never started. He has worked with us to perform a critical review of all the residual income indicators, and we have together realised the gaps in the current measures and how to bridge the gaps with new and insightful ideas and tools.

We must acknowledge our company for giving us all the opportunities to learn on the job and to build an incredible experience in the area of supply chain, project management and theoretical modelling. They have also given us the opportunity to work on this project, and to produce this summary manuscript which gathers our thinking so far.

Our invaluable collaborators in the Univesity of Cambridge — Institute for Manufacturing — have contributed to shaping the growth matrix idea and the framework for understanding and quantifying growth.

But most of all we should acknowledge our friend, mentor and business colleague, Gordon Riess MBA (a successful businessman, whose experience spans several sectors, and several continents!) for his critical review of the manuscript and for his illuminating comments and suggestions. He was indeed the first critical reader, and the first to be excited about this work. We are also indebted to Mark Cronshaw, Colorado School of

Mines — Lecturer of Economics and Business. His areas of specialisation include energy economics, microeconomics, mathematical economics, game theory, decision analysis and valuation. His careful reading of the manuscript has led to a long series of improvements.

1

DECISION UNDER UNCERTAINTY

What are you doing to improve your ability to develop and introduce new products, services, process, and strategy ideas? Are you using yesterday's methods to manage today's complex marketplace challenges?

The key business opinion leaders — the gurus of modern day — speak clearly: only companies that can consistently bring creativity, find a new way, and are able to introduce new products/services/channels, will survive and grow in today's rapidly changing market. The stock market trends reveal a consistent depression, which is the result of the frustration of most companies to turn ideas into profitable realities.

A Radical Change of Perspective

So, what is the problem? The fact is that most companies concentrate their efforts on updating the existing portfolio with only cosmetic changes, new variants, and slightly different formulations to fuel growth. In reality, this so-called *incrementalism* barely ensures survival, but does not enable sustainable growth. Surviving is not enough in today's rapidly changing market place.

So what are companies doing? Many companies are merely focussing on incremental improvement, not real breakthroughs, as managers and innovators concentrate on improving current reality. This behavior leads to short-term actions not aligned to strategy. It is like play to avoid losing!

A new *way of thinking* is needed:

• thinking the unthinkable,
• challenging the status quo, and
• taking calculated risks

will expose the new areas for opportunities. These key drivers will lead naturally towards renewed growth, profitability, management achievement, and employee satisfaction.

How can we create a new future? By defining a strategic direction to guide short- and long-term activity, focussing on creating a new paradigm, and an attitude to play to win. The growth agenda will fold out naturally — and this is what matters.

Many corporate entities are still seeking an easy way to achieve growth via mergers and acquisitions — see the recent P&G moves in acquiring Gillette, Clairol, ... and who knows what else! But is growth through mergers and acquisitions a sustainable path? We do not think so: in the limit, this path will be self-limited by anti-trust issues, by the company culture clash and by the lack of a healthy competition.

There are a number of alternative avenues available to pursue growth, which include adding new products and services and entering new markets or businesses. Yet, perhaps the most effective way to generate breakthrough and increase growth is often neglected: connecting with the consumer, and extending the customer relationship and leveraging the internal force, which is hiding inside everyone within the organisation!

In 2003 Larry Kellam, director of supply-network innovation at Procter & Gamble, stated that P&G was rethinking Supply Chain, working toward a vision called "the consumer-driven supply network." That differs from P&G supply-chain strategy of the past as consumer focussed, and it envisions a network rather than a chain. Therefore, a U-turn from the cost mentality to consumer–customer services is a must do, based on real time and all network participants working to add value for the consumer.

Consumer Driven Supply Network (CDSN) capabilities/technologies needed to implement a lean and responsive supply network are more speculative at this time. P&G paint a picture of "Flexi-plants" that react very quickly, supported by Just in Time (JIT) materials from suppliers.

Shortening end-to-end replenishment lead times ameliorates the impact of uncertainty in the supply network and reduces cycle times, enabling inventory to be taken out. But the supply network trade-offs here can be complex to quantify. P&G's approach has been to develop simulation models to show how increasing frequencies for production and transportation trade-off against inventory and service levels. P&G is investing in areas to support this direction; for example, real-time planning of the supply network is a key enabler of CDSN and underlies P&G's investment in BIOS Group and P&G's fostering a joint development between SAP and BIOS Group.

Therefore, what keeps the CEO awake at night is not only the preoccupation of reaching top and bottom line growth, but also employee and customer satisfaction. There is a new pressure coming from the world of capital markets: investors and shareholders are becoming more proactive in influencing boardrooms. This trend for investors to intervene originated in the US, but it is now spreading rapidly into the UK, European and Asian stock markets.

The pressure is now on for companies to deliver the goods. Single digit growth is not enough to satisfy the city's investors, and companies need to step-up their game to deliver year-on-year sustainable above-average returns.

Investors are becoming more and more interventionists in the management decision-making processes, once sole territory of corporate boardrooms. There is a clear message, here:

"Executives must create value or someone else will do it for them!"

The power of the capital markets is increasing over and beyond every expectation, and is setting the rules of the game in politics and in international economics. We need to buy into the new rules of the game!

The capital market 'mighties' are pushing corporations for readily available, reliable, and comparable information — so they can judge the company's performance. Why do they need this? This is to be able to make comparative judgements of a company's performance; to be able to do so across various sectors; and to be able to do so on an equitable basis. We need to develop the right tools to support comparative judgements!

The New Business Drivers

The rules that determine sustained competitive advantage and upon which superior financial results depend have shifted into a new paradigm (Donnellan, 2000). Four core beliefs have been shifted from the old to the new concepts as follows:

From	$\rightarrow$	To
Market share	$\rightarrow$	Value of market
Product Power	$\rightarrow$	Customer Power share
Revenue & P&L	$\rightarrow$	Cash
Technology	$\rightarrow$	Business design

We need a new way of thinking and making decisions that can assess the impact on the value of reducing lead-time, changing the configuration of the supply-demand chain, rationalizing the product range, or focusing on a smaller number of key customers. The approach combines the historic perspective with a predictive, forward-looking view, and also embraces the non-financial drivers of the business. It should be a systematic bridge linking executive management with front line managers out in operations. It should be a common decision-making system based upon the overarching objective of enhancing shareholder value (Rappaport, 1986).

The three most important things that you need to measure in a business are customer–consumer satisfaction, employee satisfaction, and cash flow. How do you measure customer–consumer satisfaction and employee satisfaction? What techniques should be used? Jack Welsh of G.E. said "If you cannot measure it, you cannot control it". If you are growing customer–consumer satisfaction, this is reflected in the fact that your global market share grows. This is the main output indicator to be measured — which can be combined with other specific indicators, which measure satisfaction along the value chain, such as customer surveys, service level agreements target reviews, output reliability, and so on.

Employee satisfaction gets you productivity, quality, pride, and creativity. Again, there are several ways to amplify employee satisfaction currently in use in the field, such as periodic people surveys, the merit index, and so on.

More and more companies are shying away from historic, retrospective financial reporting, and have moved to new decision support systems that are forward-looking, predictive, and responsive. This reflects what is happening in the business, and outside it, by using, for example, a combination of financial and non-financial data. Their decision-making processes are highly informed. Traditional focus on tracking budget variances, crunching the period-end numbers and preparing statutory reports is being changed. It is all about 'accounting for value' not 'accounting for profit'. Accounting for value brings absolute transparency to the hidden sources of wealth creation in the enterprise.

In benchmarking a company, analysts now compare the performance level that is being achieved against the major drivers of free cash flow (see Figure 1.1). Then they add in the benchmark of how much free cash flow per share is being generated. Executive management sees, often for the first time, just how far they are lagging behind the returns that their nearest competitors are providing to their own shareholders.

By measuring performance *ad hoc*, executive management measures the strength of the competitive fundamentals of these differing businesses and can analyze the results of the alternate strategies.

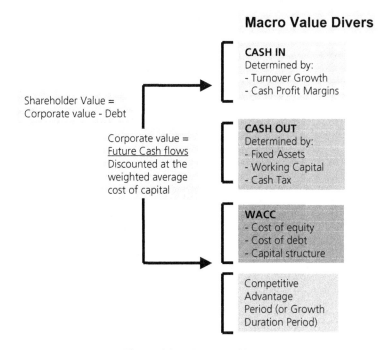

Figure 1.1. The value drivers.

But is this enough? Executive management has to be increasingly more agile in the way it responds to the changing field of competitive play on its day-to-day decisions. Management can use the same value analysis methods in a forward-looking decision-making process.

The creation of economic value tends to be a function of these value drivers.

The value chain becomes even more complex (see Figure 1.2) when taking into account the whole supply chain perspective. In reality the value is the result of a complex entanglement of easily measurable (as material costs), and not-so-easily measurable (as the supply chain responsiveness) quantities.

Efforts to "measure" supply chain performance has traditionally focused on a variety of accounting-based measures including an assortment of cost-based numbers such as inventory turnover rates, cycle-times, defect rates, and many other similar metrics. In fact, the "science" of such metrics and

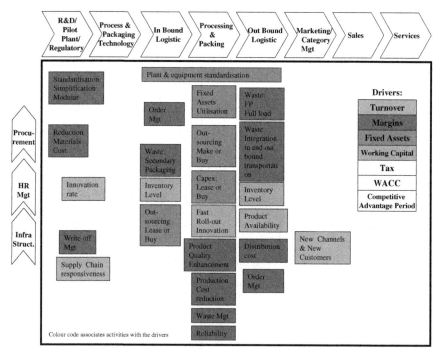

Figure 1.2. How value drivers are linked in the value chain, in a highly complex entanglement of easily and no-so-easily measurable quantities.

operation analysis has developed over time, aided more recently by the emergence of computers with the ability to crunch massive amounts of data. Operation analysts have a real-time ability to take the pulse of a company's global supply chain system on a minute-by-minute basis. Unfortunately, the ability to evaluate performance by the numbers, while saying nothing about how effectively such measurability is contributing to the creation of economic value, can satisfy the ego of keeping everything under control. This is true for several reasons.

Traditonal Accounting Measures are Surpassed

Firstly, often times the numbers are managed to mask a bad quarter or to make good numbers look even better. However, if performance is evaluated on a cash-flow basis, these distortions disappear and the focus begins to shift to the creation of economic value. These kinds of "distortions" also occur where investment in working capital and plant and equipment are concerned. For example, as a company grows sales there will normally be an associated increase in working capital. Focusing strictly on manufacturing, that means an increase in investment in cash and marketable securities to support supply chain related cash outflows and increased investment in inventory. Investment in inventory involves cash payments for materials, labor, and overheads. These cash outflows are, of course, reflected as assets on the balance sheet, but they are not included in cost-of-goods-sold, a commonly used measure for evaluating supply chain performance. Correspondingly, accounts payable represents, among other things, unpaid bills related in part to manufacturing and this tends to overstate cash outflows associated with the cost-of-goods-sold.

Plant and equipment are depreciable assets and they are accounted for at cost. This cost is allocated over the life of the asset and presumably reflects the rate at which these assets are being used up. In reality, declared depreciation almost never accurately reflects the dissipation of economic value (these assets tend to be far more valuable in productive terms than their book value suggests) and the way these assets are depreciated can dramatically affect a variety of measures commonly used to evaluate supply chain performance. Furthermore, because depreciation is a tax-deductible expenditure but is non-cash in nature, it tends to distort earnings-based measures of performance. Also, because revenue flows are not adjusted for incremental investment in plant and equipment, any earnings-based measures of supply chain performance are further distorted. This is clearly not the case if the focus is on cash flow and, correspondingly, the creation of economic value.

Secondly, accounting-based measures of supply chain performance are inadequate for judging whether a company is world-class because they ignore the time value of money. Economic value is based on the presumption that a euro of cash received today is worth more that a euro of cash received next year. And there are countless examples of "growth" companies that have invested in inventory and plant and equipment only to see sales and earnings grow and the value of the business decline. To create economic value, management must generate operating returns on invested capital that are greater (perhaps much greater) than the company's cost of capital. None of the measures commonly used to evaluate manufacturing performance effectively address this reality.

Thirdly, accounting-based measures of supply chain performance are inadequate to deal with risk. A Company's cost of capital is in reality a risk-adjusted hurdle rate that reflects the economic return demanded by investors. With this in mind, even the most casual observer would recognise immediately that none of the broadly used measures of supply chain performance, accounting based or otherwise, effectively adjusts for the risk inherent in a strategy.

Finally, the need to generate and drive growth. Enduring business success only comes from growth, consistently achieved over many years. While today's low inflation, highly competitive environment can make sustained growth more difficult to achieve, investor demands on companies to achieve growth are as insistent as ever.

The constant strive for growth

There are two key processes in the management operating system that focus on growth, which apply to every business and every market. The first process is a long-range strategic plan (envision the future). You assess your own position and that of your competitors, as well as the overall market environment, to see what kind of growth you can get. The second process focuses on identifying the key initiatives that will be needed to reach that growth target. This really helps lay out all the opportunities as to where the growth will come from.

However, these are the typically financial-based measures, but companies are also heavily assessed on culture — on values, on teamwork, on developing staff and so on. Overall performance assessment is a combination of both financial measures on one hand, and values and culture on the other.

Sometimes, the values and culture are stressed more than the financial targets. If, for example, an executive is living the values and culture, but not making the numbers, they do get more chances within the organisation. If, however, an executive is making the numbers but not upholding the culture, they do not really have a future.

There is a whole process for this — we measure it, monitor it, and reward it accordingly. You have to apply process disciplines to growth, just as you do to any other area of your business.

If growth remains the biggest challenge facing the business today, we do not lack in opportunities — from extending the core business to developing new businesses. However, to achieve a major step in growth, we need to wisely place big bets in bold innovations. Such bold moves in uncertain times with increasing stakes require us to structure our decision-making process in a way that minimises the downside whilst retaining the flexibility to exploit the upside. One can exploit traditional tools to discriminate against uncertainty. However, they do not communicate and value of 'hidden' flexibilities.

For example, Internal Rate of Return is the most commonly used tool to value opportunities. It is premised on assumptions that the decision is to be made now and future cash flows are predictable, with all the risk accounted for in the hurdle rate. It does not consider immeasurable factors, such as, benefits of qualitative/strategic positions. In reality, we make a series of decisions as we react to changes in the environment, or as we acquire new knowledge — this in effect is exercising options.

How to turn uncertainty into value

Since most business decisions are in reality about managing options, we can use options to improve decision-making under uncertainty in every business. Options are about flexibility. The greater the uncertainty, the more valuable the options become as they give flexibility to take the upside or limit the downside. In managing large innovation portfolios, we are currently faced with many options questions. We need to embed options thinking and provide options tools to help pick the winners.

The options approach to managing uncertainty involves adopting the thinking that uncertainty has value: widening the field to include other ideas could fuel other growth opportunities.

There are options in many parts of our business. The options approach can be applied in many aspects of our business:

- Marketing: managing a brand portfolio, entering new markets and alternative brand investments,
- R&D: optimum allocation that will deliver the growth agenda,
- Supply Chain: from sourcing flexibility to applying option in commodity purchasing, and
- New businesses: through acquisitions and alliances.

It is clear that we need to improve the understanding and develop tools to:

- evaluate the growth created,
- review the current tools and projects indicators in the light of the residual income indicators, and
- address the risk associated with the current strategy and implementation, and the impact of change.

We aim to enhance the decision-making component of the project evaluation process by adding new dimensions, and by including in a semi-quantitative manner strategic considerations.

We are aiming toward a new decision-making tool, which includes several components. A Residual Income financial indicator, and a Capital Scale Index, are purely based on hard cash flow estimate. Less quantifiable issues are instead summarised into two matrices leading to the Growth index and the Risk Monitor Method index.

Value generation has become a critical factor not only in project evaluation but also in strategic planning for growth. There are many forces driving a company to continually pursue higher value and to focus on bottom line delivery. These include:

- globalised competition with companies for resources and markets,
- continuing changes in customer requirements, and
- market maturity.

As a result, traditionally accepted causal business relationships (such as the direct relationship between winning orders, market share, and long-term profitability) have been fundamentally challenged. Companies need to understand the impact of value creation and appropriation of long-term market success, to understand value drivers and their interaction, and to develop evaluation tools that will guide their development.

The concept of "value" may have different meanings to various stake-holders within a company. Moreover, as companies become increasingly complex and able to pursue more value creation opportunities in increasingly an uncertain environment, it becomes more and more difficult to manage business growth and value generation in a systematic way. Currently, value research is dominated by the concepts of Value Based Management (VBM) (Arnold, 2000) or Economic Value Added (EVA), or any other Residual Income (RI) financial indicator, which emphasise quantitative calculation of value creation or measurement, and which have a background in the disciplines of microeconomics and accounting. However, these concepts have limitations, such as, the difficulty of applying quantitative methodology to real world issues and their restriction to the evaluation of historical events. As a result, RI indicators and VBM have not been successfully linked to strategic planning, and therefore, have little influence on strategic positioning and value development for the future.

How to quantify the value added by intangibles

Strategic value adding (StVA) studies (Fine, 2002) seek to identify critical determinants of strategic value assessment. However, the StVA model (Probert, 1997) largely follows the make-or-buy decision model and ignores new business propositions and strategic positioning in the value chain. The synthesis process also lacks detailed content and an implementation procedure. Thus, there are many theoretical and practical gaps-not only in establishing the interactive relationship StVA and RI, but also in the concept of StVA itself, emerging as it does from strategic management disciplines in many different schools (Scott, 1998; Botzel, 1999; Parolini, 1999; Bovet, 2000). We have clearly articulated the need for an improved decision-making process and ideally a tool that is derived from an improved philosophy of how to make a decision under uncertainty.

In this book, we propose a performance indicator, named Project-Applied Differential Operating Value Added (PADOVA), which has been derived from current best practices in business evaluation and state of the art project management literature.

There is a way to improve these financial indicators by including the impact that project lifetime, and the impact that choices/options available to the management, during the business life, have on the business plan evaluation. As examples of real options, we consider in this work the option to grow or to shrink the business activity. The improved financial indicator, named Operating Value Added (OVA), will be compared to classic indicators, such as Shareholder Value Added (SVA), and Economic Value Added (EVA).

Issues exist with the implementation of the Net Present Value (NPV) concept in project appraisal. Our purpose is to provide some theoretical background and justification for the adjustments we propose to standard NPV project appraisal methodologies. It is well documented that the application of NPV within project appraisal often involves making numerous assumptions, which ignore critical business considerations. This fact partly explains why many managers still cling to older, often more intuitive techniques, such as payback time or Internal Rate of Return (IRR) and why numerous extensions of the NPV method, such as real options, have emerged. It is generally prudent to assume a greater discount rate for portions of the project farther out in the future to account for rapidly increasing uncertainty augmented by increasing competitive and industry risk. We propose an alternative method to adjust the discount rate to correct NPV bias, which we shall name the Enhanced NPV (ENPV).

In addition, we shall discuss how to address project capital scale issues. When the size of a project's cash flows (*i.e.* project scale) can significantly alter a company's financial structure, the company's cost of acquiring debt and equity capital may increase or decrease depending on the changed risk profile. Managers often employ the Return on Investment (RoI) and other related measures, such as Return on Net Assets (RoNA) alongside the NPV technique to normalised profit indicators for project scale. However, these measures themselves do not give an adequate account of the size of the capital at risk. We shall propose an operational standalone measure, named Capital Scale Index (CSI), for the scale of capital investments.

On the other hand, business performance measurement (BPM) research has developed numerous methodologies which have been typically more qualitatively-oriented (Lynch, 1991; Kaplan, 1996) and more focused on operational efficiency (Neely, 1995). While these popular techniques in many ways address many of the shortcomings of traditional financial indicators, their application is usually on an *ex post* basis (*e.g.* operations auditing) or in a detached corporate setting (*e.g.* strategic planning).

A New Approach to Value

We propose to integrate many of these advances, as well as components from classical business strategy, directly into project evaluation to ensure *a priori* consideration of key strategic issues at the outset of each project. We also propose several ways to enhance and correct the biases of the existing residual income methodologies.

The growth index essentially attempts to capture all non-financial sources of value growth within a prospective project. Initially inspired by Fine's analogous concept of "strategic value added" (Fine, 2002), the index was entirely rebuilt based on the following considerations:

1. The need to readdress fundamental shortcomings of the residual income approach, namely issues of quantifiability, externalities, uncertainty, and path dependency
2. The need to bridge the dichotomy between value creation and appropriation, prompted by older distinctions between the resource-based view and the market-based competitive forces framework (Porter, 1980)
3. The need to jointly and proactively pursue supply chain value, operational/manufacturing value-added, and customer value (Parolini, 1999), and
4. The need to incorporate advances in Business Performance Measures into project appraisal an *a priori* basis.

We identified the value of a project to be based on two major elements:

Operational value

- Projected revenues and profits,
- Operational effectiveness — facilitates achievement of existing and potential operational requirements,
- Operational efficiency — potential for continuous improvement/cost reduction and incorporation of best practices, and
- Operational externalities — immediate synergies vis-à-vis other existing projects.

(Though the latter three are included implicitly within cash flow projections, the need to proactively manage these critical issues demands their separate treatment)

Business value

- Resource accumulation — resources accumulated yielding potential rents
- Capability development — capabilities developed impacting future projects
- Industry structure/conduct — impact on industry structure and level of competition
- Business characteristics — changes induced in key industry operating characteristics and order-qualifying/-winning criteria

We propose to evaluate these two elements on four different interrelated levels:

Process
1. Product development
2. Product delivery

Linkages
3. Customer involvement
4. Supply chain management

Decision making cannot be focused mainly on the best

- Maximum return/profit,
- Minimum cost,
- Shortest time of completion.

In supporting decision-making under uncertain conditions, the business manager needs to take into account the minimum risk. All risks must be identified and assessed to ensure that they do not adversely affect the business decisions.

Our thoughts

The proposed methodology, PADOVA is composed of four independent elements:

(1) Residual Income evaluation,
(2) Capital Scale Index,
(3) Growth Index, and
(4) Risk Index.

The overall project assessment should take into account these four different elements into the final evaluation, so that the project can be assessed from a holistic point of view. In more detail:

(1) The *Residual Income* evaluation is based on the projected cash flow of the project, where substantial improvements have been added with respect to traditional RI indicators. We have provided for:
  - (a) quantitative evaluation of **management flexibility** along the timeline of the cash flow forecast, in term of Real Options theory;
  - (b) inclusion of the **project life-time**, with the concept of the profitability parabola; and
  - (c) time variability of discount rates, and consequent increasing **forecast unreliability** at long times, in the form of an enhance NPV calculation;
(2) The *Capital Scale Index*, is a simple acid test extension aimed at promoting projects involving a **lower total capital invested** up-front.
(3) The *Growth Index* is based on two simple one-page questionnaire testing wheather the project will impinge on key **supply chain drivers or business drivers**, which are grouped along four categories: Product

15

Development, Product Delivery, Customer Involvement, and Supply Chain Management. The results are summarised into a matrix, which is organised in seven columns representing the strategic thrusts: operational effectiveness, operational efficiency, operational externalities, resource accumulation, capability development, industry structure, and business characteristics.

(4) *Risk Index* is an assessment of the risk involved in undertaking a new project and evaluating the risk of the probability of occurrence and its manageability.

Reflection on Learnings

"What three (or four) lessons have we learned?"

1. The pace of change has increased dramatically in recent times. The global dimension of information, borne out of the IT and communication (*i.e.* Internet) progress, has enabled accessibility beyond what was imaginable. Everything seems to be possible now! No rules, no barriers, and no hurdles. Fast and easy for everyone.
2. The world of business is not immune from chaos. The decision-making process needs to change in order to reflect a more complex and complicated network of opposing forces which drive the landscape of business reality today.
3. As a result, current practices and paradigms need to change in the right direction. A new way of making business decisions is needed, which builds on two concepts:

   — there is always room for improvement in current accounting measures
   — the proposed improvements should always be easy to understand and easy to implement

4. Our response to this need for change is two-fold:

   (a) a mediation between strict accounting rules and not-easy-to-measure variables, which are linked to intangibles (*e.g.* a 'quantitative value' of flexibility)
   (b) an improvement beyond the existing methods of accounting to include new concepts (*e.g.* the time-effect of profit)

"How do I put them into practical application?"

A. When making a business decision, go beyond standard pay-back time and residual income-based measures, and be open to more advanced value-based measures, which quantify not-so-easy to measure variables such as the time effect on profit, management flexibility, and so on.
B. Always balance out rigorous decision-making analysis and pragmatism.

C. At the end of the day, do not just base your business decision on a single summarising quantity, rather strive for an integrated approach that provides you with a short list of indicators (a scorecard) which is able to cover several different and complementary aspects of the same issue.

2

CRITICAL REVIEW OF
ACCOUNTING PERFORMANCE
MEASURES

Words of caution before you start reading this chapter. This section contains a review of accounting performance measures, and represents our long journey to discovering the gaps exposed in current techniques. In essence, this is a summary of our understanding of the current financial measures. It is interesting reading, but do not attempt to finish it all in one go.

Residual Income Indicators (RII) are a family of accounting performance measures defined to be operating profit subtracted with capital charge. A specific residual income indicator differs from the other with respect to different definitions of what operating profit and capital charge include. RII are not a new discovery and, indeed Shareholder Value Added (SVA), Economic Value Added (EVA), and Total Business Return (TBR) are just other varieties of residual income indicators.

Residual Income Indicators

The background of Residual Income Indicators (RII)

One of the earliest to mention the residual income concept was Alfred Marshall in 1890. Marshall defined economic profit as total net gains less the interest on invested capital at the current rate. The idea of residual income appeared first in accounting theory literature early in this century by, *e.g.* Church in 1917 and by Scovell in 1924, and appeared in management accounting literature in the 1960s.

Plenty of residual income measures exist as these are created by consulting industry and/or by academics. Consultants are forced to use a particular acronym of their concept, although it would not differ very much from the competitors'. Thus, the range of these different acronyms is wide. In the following, we mention only few of them which are relevant to our work and we refer to Makelaines (Makelaines, 1998) for a discussion of few others. We will concentrate on:

- Economic Value Added (EVA),
- Shareholder Value Added (SVA) and
- Total Business Return (TBR) indicator.

EVA (Stewart, 1990) is based on the difference between the net operating profit, and the financial cost of capital necessary to produce it. Specific adjustments are then applied, as the economic value (vs. the book value) of the accounts has to be employed. The Net Present Value (NPV) concept is then applied to the EVA generated each year to evaluate the overall business performance.

SVA origins from the discounted cash flow model. SVA discounts estimated future cash flows to present, and hence, continuously calculate the value of the company over a period of time (Rappaport, 1986). SVA has gained great publicity and an established position, although is far less used than EVA.

The TBR indicator, proposed by the Boston Consulting Group (BCG) and the Financial Yardstick Group, builds on Rappaport's SVA. Again, TBR is based on the adaptation of the discounted cash flow model.

Among the several competitors, however, EVA stands up as the most widely used residual income measure for performance evaluation. Indeed, in the 1970s or earlier, residual income measures did not get wide publicity, and they were not the prime performance measures in many companies. In recent years, the spreading of EVA and other residual income measures does not seem to be on a weakening trend. On the contrary, the number of companies adopting EVA are increasing rapidly. EVA was marketed with a concept of market value added, and it did offer a theoretically sound link to market valuations. At a time when investors demanded focus on share-holder value issues, this was a good bite. Perhaps, pertinent marketing by Stern Stewart & Co. had and has its contribution. EVA happens to be an easier implementation of residual income. In implementing EVA, one of the most important things is not only to get the people in organisations to commit to EVA but also to understand EVA. Even a concept as easy as EVA seems to be quite hard to communicate within a larger company (That is why complicated measures never work very well).

Residual income indicators vs. traditional performance measures

Residual income indicators, such as EVA, SVA and TBR, are superior than traditional accounting performance measures, such as Return on Investments (ROI), Internal Rate of Return (IRR), and so on, because they account better for the cost of the capital employed and, hence, for the risk of a company's operations. Furthermore, residual income indicators are constructed so that maximising them can be set as a target. Traditional measures do not work that way. Maximising any accounting profit or accounting rate of return leads to an undesired outcome. The following paragraphs seek to clarify the benefits of residual income measures compared to conventional performance measures, such as Net Present Value (NPV), IRR, ROI, Dividends, Return on Equity (ROE) and Earning per Share. Before diving into the discussion, a common definition for each measure is reported. While reading the following definition, keep in mind that different analysts may define terms like profit, capital, and so on in a different way depending on the situation.

ROI

$$ROI = Profits/Capital \times 100$$

NPV

The sum that results when the DISCOUNTED value of the expected costs of an investment is deducted from the discounted value of the expected returns.

$$NPV = [SUM \text{ from } t = 1 \text{ to } n \text{ of } EFCF(t)/(1 + WACC)^t]$$
$$+ TV/(1 + WACC)^n$$

where:

$$t = \text{time}$$
$$\text{EFCF}(t) = \text{Expected Free Cash Flow at period } t$$
$$\text{WACC} = \text{Weighted average cost of capital}$$
$$\text{TV} = \text{Terminal Value}$$

IRR

It is the discount rate that makes the net present value of a project equal to zero.

$$[\text{SUM from } t = 1 \text{ to } n \text{ of EFCF}(t)/(1 + \text{IRR})^t] + \text{TV}/(1 + \text{IRR})^n = 0$$

EPS

$$\text{EPS} = \text{Profit}/(\text{Number of Shares Outstanding})$$

Dividend

The amount of corporate profits to be distributed to shareholders.

ROE

$$\text{ROE} = \text{Profit}/\text{Equity Capital}$$

Discussion of NPV vs. IRR and ROI

Return on capital is very common and is a relatively good performance measure. Different companies calculate this return with different formulae and also call it with different names like ROI, Return on invested capital, Return on capital employed, Return on net assets, Return on assets, and so on. The main shortcoming with all these rates of return is that maximising rate of return does not necessarily maximise the return to shareholders in all cases. The following simple example will clarify this statement (Makelainen, 1998).

Let us consider a group with two subsidiaries; for both subsidiaries, and so for the whole group, the cost of capital is 10%. The group names maximising ROI as target. One subsidiary has ROI of 15% and the other, 8%. Both subsidiaries begin to struggle for the common target and try to maximise their own ROI. The better daughter company rejects all the projects that produce a return below their current 15%, although there would be some projects with return 12%–13%. The other affiliate, in turn, accepts all the projects with returns above 8%. For some reasons (*e.g.* over heated competition) it does not find very good projects, but the returns of its project lie somewhere near 9%.

Let us suppose that both subsidiaries manage to increase their ROI. With a better subsidiary, ROI increases from 15 to 16% and with a not-so-good subsidiary ROI increases from 8% to 8.5%. The company's target, increasing ROI, is achieved but what about the shareholder value? It is obvious that all the projects of the not-so-good subsidiary decrease the shareholder value, because the cost of capital is more than the rate of return (and so the shareholders money would have been better off with alternative investments, e.g. in the markets). But the actions of the better subsidiary are neither optimal for shareholders. Of course, shareholders will benefit not only from the good (return over 15%) projects, but also from all 12%– 13% (actually all above 10% = cost of capital) projects should have been accepted even though they decrease current ROI. These projects still create and increase shareholder value.

As the above example demonstrates, operations should not be guided with the goal to maximise the rate of return. As a relative measure and without the risk component, ROI fails to steer operations correctly. Therefore, capital can be misallocated on the basis of ROI. Firstly, ROI ignores the definite requirement that the rate of return should be at least as high as the cost of capital. Secondly, ROI does not recognise that shareholders' wealth is not maximised when the rate of return is maximised. Shareholders want the company to maximise the absolute return above the cost of capital and not to maximise percentages. Companies should not ignore projects yielding more than the cost of capital just because the return happens to be less than their current return. Cost of capital is a much more important hurdle rate than the company's current rate of return.

Observing the rate of return and making decisions only based on it is similar to assessing products on the "gross margin on sales" percentage. The product with the biggest "gross margin on sales" percentage is not necessarily the most profitable product. The product profitability also depends on the product volume. In the same way, bare high rate of return should not be used as a measure of a company's performance. Also the magnitude of operations, *i.e.* the amount of capital that produces that return is important. High return is a lot easier to achieve with tiny amount of capital than with large amount of capital. Almost any highly profitable company can increase its rate of return if it decreases its size or overlooks some good projects, which produces a return under the current rate of return.

IRR is a good way to assess investment possibilities, but we ought not prefer one investment project to the other according to their IRR. Assume two good and exclusive investment projects, Project 1 and Project 2. Project 1 has lower IRR but is much bigger in scope (bigger initial investment, bigger cash flows and bigger NPV). It (the project offering lower IRR) is better for shareholders even though it has lower IRR because it provides bigger absolute return than Project 2. The reason is exactly the same as with ROI: maximising the rate of return percentage does not matter. What matters is the absolute amount of shareholders' wealth added.

In the corporate control, it is worth remembering that EVA and NPV go hand in hand as also ROI and IRR. The formers tell us the impacts to shareholders wealth and the latter tell us the rate of return. There is no reason to abandon ROI and IRR. They are very good and illustrative measures that tell us about the rate of returns. IRR can always be used along with NPV, in investment calculations and ROI can always be used along with EVA in company performance. However, we should never aim to maximise IRR and ROI, and we should never base decisions on these two metrics. IRR and ROI provide us additional information, although all decisions could be done without them. Maximising rate of returns (IRR and ROI) does not matter, when the goal is to maximise the returns to shareholders. EVA and NPV should be in the commanding role in corporate control, and ROI and IRR should have the role of giving additional information.

Return on equity (ROE)

ROE suffers from the same shortcomings as ROI. Risk component is not included and hence there is no comparison. The level of ROE does not tell the owners if the company is creating shareholders' wealth or destroying it. With ROE, this shortcoming is however much more severe than with ROI, simply because increasing leverage can increase ROE. As we all know, decreasing solvency does not always make shareholders' position better because of the increased (financial) risk. As ROI and IRR, ROE is also an informative measure, but it should not guide the operations.

Dividends and EPS

Investing more capital in business can rise EPS. If the additional capital is equity (cash flow), then the profit (and EPS, as a consequence) will rise if the rate of return of the invested capital is just positive. If the additional capital is debt, then the profit will rise if the rate of return of the invested capital is just above the cost of debt. In reality, the invested capital is a mix of debt and equity, and the profit will rise if the rate of return of that additional capital invested is somewhere between cost of debt and zero.

Therefore, EPS is an inappropriate measure of corporate performance, but still it is a very common yardstick and even a common criterion for assigning bonus schemes. (No wonder shareholders are too fond of management bonuses.) Pouring more money into business, even though the return on that money would be entirely unacceptable from the viewpoint of owners, can increase EPS and earnings. Once again, EPS, earnings and earnings/EPS growth should not be the main guide to operations.

Three advanced residual income indicators

In the previous section, we discussed the limits of traditional performance measures, such as NPV, IRR, ROI, ROE, EPS, versus residual income measures. We will now describe three definitions for residual income measures that have been recently adopted quite successfully as measure of business performances.

In a nutshell, residual income indicators, like EVA, SVA and TBR, provide superior evaluation of business performances because they account in a better way for the cost of the capital employed and, hence, for the risk of a company's operations. Furthermore, residual income indicators are constructed so that maximising them can be set as a target. The latter does not necessarily hold for traditional — Rate of Return — performance measures.

In the following, we will discuss three residual income indicators proposed by Rappaport, Stewart and BCG, outlining their similarities and features.

Rappaport

Rappaport's Shareholder Value Added was introduced in 1986 as the present value of the operating cash flow plus the present value of the residual value of a business, possibly adjusted to consider marketable securities, minus the corporate debt. The formulae are:

$$\text{Shareholder Value (SV)} = \text{Corporate Value} - \text{Debt}$$
$$\text{Corporate Value} = \text{PV(Cash flow)} + \text{PV(Residual Value)}$$
$$+ \text{Marketable securities}$$

where

PV(...) stands for the calculation of the present value.

The SV indicator rests on the concept of operating cash flow, which could be known from the operating company report sheet. The cash flow for the forecast years is discounted according to the weighted average cost of capital (K), in order to calculate its present value.

The next step is the calculation of market value of the business at the end of the forecast period. Here a simple perpetuity model is used in order to project the predicted cash in-flow into the future. The same cost of capital is used to calculate the present value of the market value. The definition for the terms involved in the SV definition are as follows:

$$\text{Cash flow} = \text{NOPAT} - \text{Incremental fixed plus working capital}$$
$$\text{investment}$$
$$\text{NOPAT} = (\text{Sales in prior year})(1 + \text{Sales growth rate})$$
$$\times (\text{Operating profit margin})(1 - \text{Cash income tax rate})$$
$$\text{Residual Value} = \text{NOPAT}/K$$
$$\text{PV(Residual Value)} = (\text{NOPAT}/K)/(1 + K)^n$$
$$\text{PV(Cash flow)} = \text{SUM } t = 1 \text{ to n of Cash flow}(t)/(1+K)^t$$

Finally, Rappaport defines the amount of wealth created as SVA:

$$\text{Corporate Value} = \text{PV(Cash flow)} + \text{PV(Residual Value)}$$
$$+ \text{Marketable securities}$$
$$\text{Shareholder Value} = \text{Corporate Value} - \text{Debt}$$
$$\text{Shareholder Value Added} = \text{PV(Cash flow)} + \text{PV(Residual Value)}$$
$$+ \text{Residual Value}_0$$

where NOPAT_0 represents the NOPAT of the prior year.

The SVA over one year is then the difference between the present value of the last year cash flow and the present value of the business residual value, minus the prior year business residual value.

Stewart

Stewart proposes to evaluate a company performance over a period of time in terms of cash inflow or Net Operating Profit After Taxes (NOPAT), and cash outflow or cost of the capital employed by the company. The measure used to assess a company's performance is known as Economic Value Added (EVA), as it measures the wealth created by the business over a period of time.

Over a one year period, a company's performance or EVA results are as follows:

$$\text{EVA} = \text{NOPAT} - \text{Cost of Capital}$$

where,

$$\text{Cost of Capital} = \text{Weighted Averaged Cost of Capital (WACC)}$$
$$\times \text{Adj Corp Capital}$$
$$\text{Adj Corp Capital} = \text{Debt} + \text{Equity} + \text{Def Income taxes} + \text{Lifo Reserve}$$
$$+ \text{Acc Goodwill Amort} + \cdots$$

The definition of the cash inflow as NOPAT is widely employed by many authors, so no further discussion is worthwhile. On the contrary, Stewart's definition of the cash outflow as the Cost of Capital represents a departure from other approaches. According to Stewart, after a company has been able to pay back the financial cost of the capital employed, the remaining cash represents the newly created wealth. No information based on the operating costs, i.e. about the way the corporate capital is employed in the business, is taken into account to calculate the cash outflow. Instead, the market is made king. Indeed, the market law will change the WACC depending on how well the business is managed.

If EVA really measures how much wealth a company creates, it should be somehow linked to its market value, especially in case of a listed company.

Indeed, Stewart introduces other two measures: Market Value (MV), accounting for the market appreciation for a business and Market Value Added (MVA), accounting for the wealth created over the book value of equity. Then Stewart shows their links with EVA.

For sake of simplicity, considering a 1-year period, the following relationships hold:

$$MVA = EVA/(1 + WACC)$$

$$MV \sim MVA + (\text{Book value of Equity}$$
$$+ \text{Book Value of Equity Equivalents})$$

and also:

$$MV = n^o \text{ of outstanding shares} \times \text{one share market price}$$

The main idea underlying Stewart's approach is that, any variation between a company market value (MV), its Book Value of Equity and Equity Equivalents represents the creation or the destruction of wealth caused by the company management. This difference corresponds to the NPV of EVA over the considered period.

It is important to note that the NPV of EVA is equal to MVA or a good approximation of it, if the future business performance is being properly forecasted or if the past business performance in the stock market has been compared to the NPV of EVA. The value of a business in the stock market may also be dependent on contingent reasons based perhaps on fad rather than financially grounded arguments. Be the 1999 stock market bubble for Internet companies is an example of such irrational market behaviour.

TBR (Total Business Return)

TBR indicator, produced by the Boston Consulting Group (Warner A., 2001), is based on the discounted cash flow notion and the full market model developed by the Financial Yardstick Review team. TBR builds on Rappaport's idea of cumulative discounted free cash flow.

The starting point is the operating cash flow, as defined in standard financial terms.

$$OCF = NOPAT - (\text{Incremental fixed and working capital investment})$$

where,

NOPAT is the Net Operating Profit After Taxes.

For the discounting procedure TBR uses an effective value, after tax, in our specific case we have used a rate of 6%, which is considered to be the weighted average cost of capital. The present value of the operating cash flows is cumulated for all the forecast years. For sake of simplicity, we shall write the explicit formulae for a 1-year period:

$$OCF = NOPAT - (\text{Incremental fixed plus working capital investment})$$
$$NOPAT = (\text{Sales in prior year})(1 + \text{Sales growth rate})$$
$$\times (\text{Operating profit margin})(1 - \text{Cash income tax rate})$$
$$PV(OCF) = \text{Cash flow}/(1 + K)$$

The next step is the calculation of the market value of the business at the beginning and at the end of the forecast years. This is done via a simple

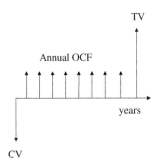

Figure 2.1. Graphical representation of current, terminal and plan value. In this picture an up-arrow represent a positive cash-flow and a down-arrow a negative one. Here we portray an arbitrary scenario where there is an initial substantial investment (CV), a constant revenue stream for the following 8 years generating a positive operating cash flow, and a final positive terminal value (TV).

perpetuity model where a constant free cash flow is projected to infinity. TBR authors rewrite the free cash flow (FCF) in our specific case accounting terms, and apply the model to the historical performance, in order to fit a couple of adjustable parameters. The result is a simple, *ad hoc*, formula for the evaluation of the market value:

$$MV = (\text{Trading Contribution} \times \text{Growth Multiple}) + 1.15 \text{ GCE}$$

where, Trading Contributions follows the specific accounting definition for the 'bottom line', Growth Multiple includes the WACC, the growth factor, and the fading factor (a rate that limits the earnings of the business in a competitive environment), GCE is the Gross capital employed.

The MV at the end of the forecast period is called Terminal Value (TV), and it needs to be discounted back at the present time using the same approximation of the cost of capital WACC. The MV at the beginning of the forecast period is called Current Value (CV). Considering a 1-year forecast period, the TV must be discounted back at WACC rate:

$$PV(TV) = TV/(1 + K)$$

The combination of the three terms, discounted operating cash flows plus present value of TV at the end minus CV, at the beginning of the forecast period, represent the Value Creation (VC):

$$VC = PV(TV) + \text{Discounted OCF} - CV,$$

The Total Business Return (TBR) indicator is then the discount rate which when applied to the calculation of total plan value in place of 6%, makes the total plan value equal to the current value:

$$PV(TV) + \text{Discounted OCF} = CV$$

Similarities and differences

In the following section we shall try to concentrate on the similarities and the main differences existing between the three residual income indicators we have defined in the previous section.

All of them are based on the concept of discounting the year-on-year residual income (based on the OCF, or some other definition of the cash flow), in order to calculate the cumulative net present value for all the years during the forecast period.

In a similar way, the three methods estimate the market value at the end of the forecast year just by calculating into perpetuity either the expected NOPAT, FCF, or the EVA. The TV is then discounted back, according to the same WACC in order to calculate its NPV.

The three methods also concentrate on the current value of the business, by using a perpetuity model of some definition of cash flow.

We can summarise the previous concepts schematically in Table 2.1.

By looking more in detail into the way the forecast period is calculated, we stress that the cash flow in the three cases is calculated in slightly different ways. Rappaport and TBR use the standard financial definition of Operating Cash Flow, while Stewart defines a new quantity, which assumes the special name of EVA. These cash flows are nevertheless calculated as a 'residual income measure', where we can identify an 'in-flow' contribution and an 'out-flow' term.

In all of them, the in-flow contribution is the standard NOPAT, which is clearly of operational origin. It is known from the published report sheets of companies, or it can be estimated as explained in the previous sections.

The 'out-flow' term, on the other hand, is different in the models considered. Rappaport and TBR consider, once again, an operational measure; the Incremental fixed plus working capital investment. Stewart chooses a financial perspective, and estimates the out-flow contribution as the Cost of Capital. According to Stewart, after a company has been able to pay back the financial cost of the capital employed, the remaining cash represents the newly created wealth.

In summary, we can gather schematically these similarities and differences in Tables 2.2–2.4:

Table 2.1. Comparison of the main components in the calculation of the total economic value measures.

	Rappaport	**Stewart**	**TBR**
Current value	Perpetuity of NOPAT	Share price	Perpetuity of FCF
Forecast Period	Discounted OCF	Discounted EVA	Discounted OCF
Terminal value	Perpetuity of NOPAT	Perpetuity of EVA	Perpetuity of FCF

Table 2.2. Comparison of different decisions.

	Rappaport	Stewart	TBR
In-flow	NOPAT	NOPAT	NOPAT
Out-flow	Incremental investment	Cost capital employed	Incremental investment
Residual income	OCF	EVA	OCF

Table 2.3. Comparison of different origins.

	Rappaport	Stewart	TBR
In-flow	NOPAT	NOPAT	NOPAT
Origin	Operational	Operational	Operational
Out-flow	Incremental investment	Cost capital employed	Incremental investment
Origin	Operational	Financial	Operational

Table 2.4. Nomenclature.

	Rappaport	Stewart	TBR
Residual income	OCF	EVA	OCF
Current value	SV_0	MV_0	CV
Terminal value	SV_1	MV_1	TV
Value created	SVA	MVA	VC
Incr value created	SVA	EVA	

In order to orient ourselves among the different definitions used by the three authors referring, essentially, to the same or very similar quantities, we provide here a schematic legend, which clarifies the different nomenclature used and direct the reader towards the right symbols and acronyms.

Shortcomings

We shall now concentrate on the similarities and the main differences existing between the residual income indicators we have defined in the previous section. All of them are based on the concept of discounting the year-on-year residual income (based on the OCF, or some other definition of the cash flow), in order to calculate the cumulative NPV for all the years during the forecast period.

Time Issues

It is well-documented that the application of NPV within project appraisal often involves making numerous assumptions, which ignore critical business considerations. This fact partly explains why many managers still cling on to older, often more intuitive techniques such as payback or IRR and why numerous extensions of the NPV method such as real options have emerged. How do you compare two projects of Unequal Project Length?

Due to the fact that the NPV represents discounted cash flow in a single summation, it is unable to differentiate between projects of different lengths. When two exclusive projects exhibit the same positive NPV, a shorter project should be preferred because the company would generally have opportunities to invest in similar projects yielding further positive NPV at the end of the shorter project. Two procedures are used to make this often-ignored distinction (Besley, 1999).

The *Replacement Chain (Common Life) Approach* assumes each project can be replicated as many times as necessary, to reach a common life span. The NPVs over this life span are then compared, and the project with the higher common life NPV is chosen. For example, when comparing a 3-year and a 5-year project, the projects will be replicated 5 and 3 times respectively, to generate 15-year life projects, whose NPVs will then be compared. A problem with this approach, however, is the difficulty decision-makers would encounter when there are numerous projects simultaneously under consideration, as this is generally the case within large multinationals.

The *Equivalent Annual Annuity Approach* converts the projects' cash flows into an equivalent annuity (constant stream of annual payments based on the NPV and discount rate) over the life of the project. The project with higher annual annuity payments would then be selected. The drawback of this method is that it is less intuitive and often too cumbersome for managers to use.

Due to the above-mentioned drawbacks, most managers fail to apply these adjustments, which leads to an NPV method which systematically, and incorrectly, biases towards longer projects. Managers have traditionally employed payback concurrently with the NPV to ameliorate this bias, leading to potential conflicting information.

Reinvestment rate

Even with equal lengths, *mutually exclusive* projects (usually the case in capital-constrained companies or when evaluating projects competing to achieve similar goals) that present different timing of cash flows can again lead to bias, through NPV's assumptions regarding the reinvestment rate of cash inflows over the project lifetime. The NPV method assumes that cash flows can only be reinvested at the required rate of return (*i.e.* the discount rate). Other techniques, such as the IRR method, imply the company has the opportunity to reinvest at the project's IRR. It is more realistic to assume that it is neither feasible nor possible to reinvest in another project with an identical IRR, and so the NPV method is a more prudent approach.

However, a caveat exists when this logic is applied to capital-constrained companies. The larger the company, the more the scope and opportunities for growth. And when the company is facing capital constraints, it is more likely that attractive alternatives (offering similar returns) to the project remain unselected. Furthermore, projects offering superior returns may arise in the future, which a capital-constrained company may prove unable to undertake. This suggests the need to arrive at an opportunity cost-based (or best alternative) calculation for the assumed reinvestment rate for project cash flow, which will most likely be somewhere between the IRR and the discount rate. Furthermore, the farther the project extends, the more likely an unidentified, superior alternative may arise, and the higher such opportunity costs may be. A failure to make this adjustment, would lead to a project evaluation process systematically biased toward long-term projects.

Non-constant accumulation of project risk

A third timing issue with NPV is its assumption of a constant accumulation of project risk, represented as a constant discount rate throughout the life of the project. Corporate experience and recent management literature suggest that the likelihood of disruptive technologies and organised competitive response, as well as the pace of product obsolescence, accelerates over the life of most projects. This leads to a supra-linear growth of project risk and cash flow uncertainty over time, which the existing NPV methodologies again underestimate.

Rapid project execution is a vital source of competitive advantage, both in terms of reducing the degree of entry barriers necessary to sustain project profitability, and by providing greater tolerance and flexibility in the face of market uncertainty. By the same logic, long-life projects should be more heavily discounted because they face threats from a wider set of market threats.

Though on the surface this seems to contradict financial dogmas, many authors have attempted to address this limitation of the NPV method. Brealey and Myers (Brealey, 1991) state that although the NPV procedure usually assumes that beta (which measures how the discount rate deviates from the risk free rate) is constant over a project's entire life, yet "there's no law of nature stating that certainty equivalents have to decrease in this smooth and regular way." They go on to say that while "it makes sense to use a single risk-adjusted discount rate as long as the project has the same market risk at each point in its life," one needs to adjust for exceptions, where market risk changes as time passes.

It is therefore possible in the application of NPV technique during project evaluation to vary the discount rate over the life of the project (Damodaran, 2001). Damodaran illustrated how "technologic uncertainty" associated with an industry can lead to higher discount rates in the later years of a project.

Time-varying discount rates

One of the ways the authors have addressed this last issue, is to reformulate NPV:

$$\text{NPV of Project} = \frac{CF_1}{(1 + r_1)} + \frac{CF_2}{(1 + r_1)(1 + r_2)}$$

$$+ \cdots + \frac{CF_n}{(1 + r_1)(1 + r_2)(1 + r_3) \cdots (1 + r_n)}$$

$$- \textit{Initial Investment}$$

Where,

CF_t = Cash flow in period t

r_t = One-period discount rate that applies to period t

n = Life of the project

Under this formulation, the discount rate r_t may vary for numerous reasons, including:

(1) The level of interest rates may change over time.
(2) The risk characteristics of the project may be expected to change in a predictable way over time.
(3) The financing mix for the project may change over time, resulting in changes in both the cost of equity and the cost of capital.

Time-varying discount rate components

The discount rate is mainly based by the cost of capital for the project, usually calculated through the WACC of the company. This is in turn dependent on the cost of equity and the cost of debt. While the cost of equity takes into consideration a number of risk factors illustrated below, the cost of debt is dependent mainly on the risk of default and the risk-free rate.

A company's cost of debt is determined by a combination of the risk-free rate (*i.e.* time value of money) and the company's perceived risk of default. Depending on the size of the project relative to the parent company, the method (financing mix) through which the project raises funds, the nature of a project's cash flows, and the expected level and stability of returns, the cost of debt facing a particular project may differ. And differences may continue to emerge throughout the life of the project, as its risk characteristics change. For example, a project with a large cash outflow in its third year may incur significantly a higher cost of debt after that date due to the company having to assume a higher leverage. This suggests that the initial stages of a project, before significant financial commitments, may be discounted less heavily than future more cash-hungry portions of the project, which may result in a higher cost of debt.

Although, when maximising shareholder value, a company should ideally only use the risk-free rate and beta risk in setting hurdle rates for projects, in reality most companies also examine the corporate risk and project-specific risk. There is good justification for this. When a company or a project exhibit high likelihood of failure, risk-averse managers, employees, suppliers and customers, often shy away from staying or dealing with the company, which can dramatically reduce the company's ability to create value. As a result, most companies adjust their discount rates (or hurdle rates) during project evaluation to incorporate potential changes.

Each of these risks needs to be evaluated during the project evaluation process to see whether the discount rate should be held constant:

- Time value of money — investor sentiment may favour more cash holdings or leverage.
- Inflation — the inflation rate may change.
- Government interest rates — government monetary policy may change.
- Market risk — a project's beta may shift during different stages of operation, or as certain economic factors become more significant.
- Corporate risk — a project's impact on a company's overall financial position can be expected to change over time, especially when the project's cash flows may represent a large portion of the company's financial position, and when the company is facing financial constraints or increasing marginal cost of capital.
- Project risk — a project's risk characteristics can be expected to change over various stages of its lifecycle. For example, the primary source of risk during product introduction may be customer acceptance, while it may be erosion of brand equity and commoditisation mature products. Different sources of risk may impact the cash flow to varying extents.

Further analysis divides various types of risks into the following categories below:

For the discount rate to hold constant in each of these categories, risk would need to accumulate steadily over time. Again, no evidence exists which shows this to be the case. Indeed, consequences of project planning miscalculations can be expected to propagate supra-linearly, as with the bull-whip effect in manufacturing. As mentioned previously, numerous authors have also noted the accelerating pace of globalised competition which affects both competitive and industry risk.

Furthermore, since each of these risk evaluations are forecasts and estimates themselves, their reliability cannot be assumed to remain constant or even degrade linearly over time, and in fact it should be assumed to decline

Table 2.5. An analysis of risk.

Type of Risk	Examples	Company Can Mitigate by	Investor Can Mitigate by	Effect on Analysis
Project-specific	– Estimation mistakes – Errors specific to product or location	– Taking a large number of projects	– Holding diversified portfolios	– Diversifiable
Competitive	– Unexpected response or new product/service from competitor	– Acquiring competitors	– Investing in the equity of competitors	– Diversifiable
Industry	– Changes that affect all companies in a industry – Divided into technology, legal/regulatory and commodity risk	– Diversifying into other businesses through acquisitions/investments	– Holding a portfolio diversified across industries	– Diversifiable
International	– Currency changes – Political changes	– Investing in multiple countries/currencies	– Holding a portfolio diversified across countries	– Diversifiable
Market/Macro	– Interest rate changes – Inflation changes – Economy			– Not Diversifiable

dramatically with time (especially when forecast horizons extend beyond typical 5-year macroeconomic models and the duration of a typical product lifecycle).

Although there are instances where risk is mitigated during a project, the above arguments suggest that it is generally more prudent to assume a greater discount rate for portions of the project farther out into the future, to account for rapidly increasing uncertainty augmented by increasing competition. We propose an alternative method for adjusting the discount rate to correct NPV bias in the following pages.

Terminal value calculation

One last timing issue stems from the application of the NPV concept within Rappaport's SVA and Stewart's EVA methodologies. When calculating the terminal value of a project, the standard applications of the NPV method (Rappaport's SVA and Stewart's EVA) both use a constant perpetuity model in estimating the project cash flows after the evaluation period. This again is unrealistic for most industry projects, where revenues decline steadily toward zero over time. We propose in the following chapters a way to go beyond this assumption.

Capital Scale Issues

Yet another limitation of the NPV methodology, is its inability to consider project scale. Using a typical rate of return estimate, which is itself based on an NPV calculation of the cumulative returns, a €1000 investment with cumulative return of €200, would share the same risk as a €100 investment with a return of €20. In fact in most cases, when setting up a partnership between two companies, the two parties agree on the same rate of return, irrespective of the different capital invested by the two different sides. While this is theoretically sound for companies with unlimited capital and zero default risk, in real life most companies face short-term capital constraints and increasing marginal costs of capital associated with default risk, stemming from higher leverage ratios and large projects. Therefore, the return on investment and business risk associated with project scale are critical project considerations.

When the size of a project's cash flows (*i.e.* project scale) can significantly alter a company's financial structure, the company's cost of acquiring debt and equity capital may increase or decrease depending on the changed risk profile. Where this changed cost of capital has significant impacts on the discounting of other projects, the effect should be included in the project evaluation as a form of synergy. Where the changes affect the cost of capital for the project itself, they should be included in the discount rate (perhaps as a time-varying discount rate described above). If these effects are not included in the project evaluation, the standard NPV methodology may be systematically biased towards large projects with one-off terminal payments, as opposed to smaller projects with frequent cash flows. Yet, such attempts are often difficult due to the indirect nature of the financial impact.

Managers often employ the Return on Investment (ROI), and other related measures, alongside the NPV technique to normalise profit indicators for project scale. However, these measures themselves do not give an adequate account of the size of the capital at risk.

To adjust the NPV for these shortcomings, we propose a stand-alone measure for the scale of capital investments.

Implications

The ideal solution for adjusting NPV techniques for scale and timing issues would be to formulate competing business plans with a long-term (20+ year) horizon. These business plans would need to be comprehensive, detailing the timing and requirements of project cash flows for any chosen project mix, the sources and likely costs of capital, and the anticipated risks. As long as business plans incorporate all possible combinations of projects and accurately assess cash flows, costs of capital and risks, finding the optimal project mix should be straightforward. Unfortunately, this is usually not feasible for large multinationals. The complexity and uncertainty of operations often limit the planning process to evaluate a limited set of scenarios and project mixes.

What we are left with, is an NPV-based project evaluation process which requires numerous adjustments for properly addressing scale and timing uses, each of which render the method too complicated for application by everyday decision-makers.

Reflection on Learnings

"What three (or four) lessons have we learned?"

1. Residual income indicators are a family of accounting performance measures defined to be the operating profit subtracted with capital charge.
2. A specific residual income indicator differs from the other with respect to different definitions of what operating profit and capital charge include. They are not a new discovery and, indeed, Shareholder Value Added (SVA), Economic Value Added (EVA), and Total Business Return (TBR) are three main examples.
3. Residual income indicators (RII), are superior to traditional accounting performance measures, like Return on Investment (ROI) or Internal Rate of Return (IRR), because they account for the cost of the capital employed and, hence, for the risk of a company's operations.

"How do I put them into practical application?"

(A) RIIs are not perfect, but are a step forward from traditional accounting performance measures, like ROI or IRR. They are constructed so that, maximising them can be set as a business target.
(B) The application of Net Present Value (NPV) within project appraisal often involves making numerous assumptions, which ignore critical business considerations. So don't believe that one number alone.

3

CRITICAL REVIEW OF STRATEGIC CRITERIA

Financial project evaluation metrics often ignore or fail to capture key considerations in corporate strategy, leading to a mismatch between strategic planning and actual operations. This arises from the inability of conventional techniques (based on discounted cash flow) to capture qualitative issues, such as flexibility and externalities whose complexity, indirect impact and uncertainty makes them difficult to incorporate into financial measures.

Shortcomings of Existing Methodology

Two popular financial evaluation methods, Rappaport's Shareholders Value Added (SVA) and Stewart's Economic Value Added (EVA), both use discounted cash flow to arrive at the Net Present Value of a project. These two models are based on the following variables:

(1) Anticipated cash inflow/revenues
(2) Anticipated cash outflow/costs/investments
(3) Discount rate or cost of capital
(4) Estimated revenue growth
(5) Tax regime

Each of these five variables is estimated using forecasts, historical figures and, where necessary, intuition.

Conventional financial analysis has four major weaknesses when applied to major investments in technological change. The first is mis-assessment of the appropriate weighted average cost of capital and discount rate, resulting into real hurdle rate which is higher than optimal, causing under investment. A second major factor is undue optimism in projecting continuing stable returns under the "no investment" alternative. A third area is concerned about "intangible" versus "tangible" benefits. Finally, we note the importance of giving explicit attention to often overlooked spin-off benefits of technology investment.

We have constructed a similar matrix categorising the various potential impacts of a project according to:

(1) Quantifiability — the impact can be measured in terms of cash flows, or it is difficult to express through cash flows (learning, technology, resources, competitive position, market access, loyalty, etc.)
(2) Uncertainty — the impact is consistent, well-known and estimable, or stochastic and intractable to calculation.
(3) Externalities — the impact is well-contained within the project at hand or has potential to enhance (or damage) the value provided through other projects.
(4) Path-dependency — current decisions limits/generates numerous unique opportunities or has little future impact.

Financial measures can deal with these potential impacts to a limited degree. Uncertain outcomes can be simplified into probabilistic averages, as well as risk aversion and expected utility functions.

Externalities can be internalised through modifying the future cash flow to include the impact on other projects. Path-dependency is resolved by assuming that the company will only make the choice which maximise profits each time. However, the difficulty of reliably forecasting and esti-mating financial variables increases exponentially with more uncertainty, externalities and path-dependency. Very quickly, bounded rationality and computational limitations require managers to employ evaluation criteria beyond readily identifiable cash flows.

As a result, projects which may have a lot of potential to generate value, but whose outcome is impossible to estimate accurately, will tend to be skewed by managers in favour of 'safer' projects with a clear bottom line, often due to corporate conservatism, managerial self-preservation, or simply a need to satisfy short-term shareholder interests. Similarly, projects with significant benefits that spill over onto other projects and/or other divisions may not be the same priority as those with more direct impact. Lastly, projects, which provide flexibility or otherwise generate/facilitate potential business/cost savings instead of direct profits, are vital to corporate growth, but may be difficult to justify financially. Financial indicators, though useful as benchmarks, do not give managers access to the strategic levers available to a company to realise potential value or improve existing returns.

For example, Rappaport (1986) lists seven 'value drivers': sales growth rate, operating profit, margin, income tax rate, fixed and working capital investment, cost of capital and value growth duration, but they are not formulated for an internal appraisal of a specific new offering.

This is why strategic considerations need to be employed to complement existing financial or residual-income-based measures.

Strategic Issues

Numerous schemes have been offered to complement traditional finance-oriented corporate decision-making. These are generally based on two major schools of strategy: Porter's competitive forces framework (Porter, 1980) and the resource-based perspective (Wenerfelt, 1984) emphasise the careful selection or positioning of a company's activities to best exploit either industry structure (to gain monopoly rents) or accessible resources and capabilities. Insights from these schemes can be used to clarify the indirect, intangible, and hard-to-measure sources of value in a project, and ensure a 'strategic fit'.

Reimann (1987) offered a strategy assessment guide which asked the manager to measure the market/industry attractiveness (based on Porter's Competitive Forces framework) and the company's relative competitive position, as a complement to the standard financial analysis, in order to fully account for strategic considerations which may influence the financial projections:

Part I. Market/Industry Attractiveness

A. Industry factors

- Absolute market size
- Market growth
- Price sensitivity
- Entry barriers (scale economies, capital investment, brand loyalty, entrenched advantages, signs of recent or potential entry, etc.)
- User negotiating power (relative size and concentration, switching costs, backward integration, importance of product to user, etc.)
- Supplier negotiating power (similar to above, in reverse)
- Substitution threats (can products or services from outside industry satisfy some or all of buyer needs)
- Competitive rivalry (concentration of competitors, generic strategies, capacity utilisation, barriers to exit, etc.)

B. Environmental factors

- Governmental regulations (product safety, pollution, OSHA, etc.)
- Economic climate (inflation, business cycle, interest rates, etc.)
- Global (foreign competition, export/imports, exchange rates, etc.)
- Social trends (demographics, social values and more, etc.)
- Other factors (e.g. technological developments)

Part II. Competitive position

A. Competitive Strength

- Current market share and trend
- Profitability and cash flow
- Differentiation
- Relative cost position

B. Sustainability of competitive advantages

- Raw materials
- Input logistics
- Output logistics
- Marketing and sales

- Services
- Customer image
- Support activities
- Other (e.g. technology, information systems administration)

John Kay (1993) identified several steps to achieving high added value:

(1) Put together a set of relationships, contractual and informal, which permits a company to co-operate co-ordinate and differentiate optimally.
(2) Ensure that these relationships bestow distinct capabilities, which resist competition. Kay lists four ways this may be achieved:

- **Architecture** — network of relational contracts with and among employees (internal architecture), with suppliers and customers (external architecture), or among a group of companies engaged in related activities (networks). This network then permits the creation of organisational knowledge and routines, responding flexibly to changing circumstances, and achieving easy and open exchanges of information.
- **Reputation** — the most important mechanism for conveying information, such as quality, performance and risk to consumers. Though difficult and costly to create, once established can yield substantial added value.
- **Innovation** — Consistently innovating, followed by the ability to implement and appropriate returns (via standards, patents, etc.) from the innovations, can be a source of sustainable competitive advantage.
- **Strategic assets** — market position or dominance based on natural monopoly, high entry costs, or market restrictions which are the products of licences and regulation.

(3) Matching and exploiting these relationships and distinct capabilities in suitable markets to achieve competitive advantage and added value.

Normann and Ramirez (1994) proposed in their ground-breaking work *Designing Interactive Strategy*, that companies should treat their industry and suppliers as part of an integrated value-creating network. Instead of ·being concerned about identifying and fulfilling customer needs, 'value constellations' built on innovative co-productive relationships will instead be reconfigured around identifying and offering activities which complement customers' activity processes through customising the range, time span, options (offering density; bundling), and risk of the offering according to the customer's preferences.

Doz and Hamel (1998) carried this idea further by proposing that finding strategically compatible partners/suppliers, and engaging in successful collaborative alliances, can be critical to issues beyond the product offering, such as learning and market access. They outlined three main forms of alliances, co-option alliances, co-specialisation alliances and learning alliances, emphasising that each carried unique evaluation criteria for success.

A key concept is strategic synergy, which focuses on the benefits derived from horizontal relationships across business activities. Different authors have different definitions of the concept. Ansoff (1968) defined synergy as the sharing of intangible assets, such as expertise or image across a portfolio and also the gains from economies of scale. Others tend to view it as the simultaneous exploitation of valuable internal resources in different end products or businesses.

Sutton (1998) proposed three core elements of modern strategic thought:

(1) **Focus** — a company needs to concentrate on what it does best, and adopt highly consistent strategies.
(2) **Flexibility** — a company needs to be responsive to change, engaged in a process of continuous transformation and innovation, and aim for market creation rather than market share.
(3) **Future development** — a company needs to be forward-looking, by challenging the rules of engagement, redrawing market boundaries or creating new industries. Future leadership requires current action to understand the trends and discontinuties, which will create new strategic space; to develop competencies; to attract coalition partners; to create infrastructures; and to provide products and services concepts customers will favour.

Fine (1998, 2002) proposed the necessity to harmonise investment and other corporate decisions within what he termed the "FAT 3-DCE Decision Model" reported in the following pages.

Table 3.1. FAT 3-DCE decision model.

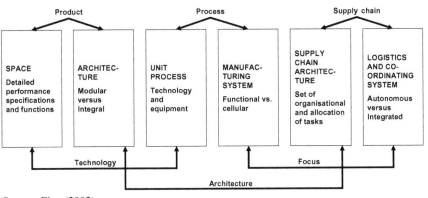

Source: Fine (2002).

Concepts such as the Value Delivery System (Lanning, 1998) and Value Net (Parolini, 1999) focus on establishing an intimate relationship with customers to identify and shape customer wants, and tailoring a closely aligned business system, which captures as much of the resulting customer value as possible.

Hax and Wilde (2001) proposed the 'Delta' business model, which outlined three distinct strategic options, and emphasised harmonisation of investments and operations to best achieve one of these:

(1) **System Lock-In** — competition based upon system economics, such as complementor lock-in, competitor lock-out and proprietary standards.
(2) **Total Customer Solutions** — competition based upon customer economics, such as reducing customer costs or increasing their profits.
(3) **Best Product** — competition based upon product economics, such as low cost or differentiation.

Fine suggested a strategic value assessment model to complement the EVA approach in making supply chain outsourcing decisions. It considered:

(1) **Customer Importance** — how each sourcing decision affects customer preferences
(2) **Technology Clockspeed** — how rapidly the underlying technology is changing

(3) **Competitive Position** — how the company compares to its competition in cost, quality and other dimensions
(4) **Supply-base Capability** — how deep and capable is the outside supply base
(5) **Architecture** — how integral or modular is the value-chain element to the architecture of the overall product, service or system

Each of these three strategic options entails a different set of performance metrics. In some cases, there will be one or two outstanding order-winning criteria, which companies can target through the development and use of core capabilities. However, in most cases, this set of strategic considerations evolves over time, and need to be weighed and balanced against each other and against financial returns.

Impact on Residual Income Indicators

Strategic considerations not only impact future cash flows, but also more specifically, impact the *planning period*, or the duration over which positive cash flows are generated. In other words, while financial analysis might calculate the magnitude of income and point out the need to reduce product and capital costs or increase revenues, strategic analysis is necessary to calculate the duration of that income.

A Three-step process can be used to link customer value to shareholder value,

(1) Determine how well you currently meet the customer's shifting price, product, and non-product needs (diagnosis)
(2) Build precision strategies that do a superior job of meeting these needs profitably (bridge)
(3) Make sure the strategies create enough customer and shareholder value to make them work (payoff)

Though they indicated the paramount importance of product quality/performance, they stop short of actually linking financial indicators to customer value. Indeed, they propose that well-planned and well-integrated strategies serves to keep prices, costs, and hence profits in line once the product offering is determined.

Table 3.2. "Delta" business model.

		Strategic Positioning		
		Best product	**Total customer solutions**	**System lock-in**

Adaptive Process	**Operational effectiveness (cost drivers)**	• Cost performance
		  – Unit cost
		  – Life cycle cost
		  – Variable and total cost
		• Cost drivers
		• Quality performance
		• Degree of differentiation
			• Customer value chain
			  – Total cost
			  – Total revenue and profit
			• Customer economic drivers
			• Impact on customer profit due to our service vs. competitors
				• Description of system infrastructure
				• Total system costs/ revenues
				• Complementors investments and profits
				• Complementors costs of adhering to your standard
				• System performance drivers

	Customer Targeting (profit drivers)	• Product market share
		• Channel cost
		• Product profit
		  – By product type
		  – By offer
		  – By channel
		• Profit drivers
			• Customer share
			• Customer retention
			• Our profitability by customer
			  – Individual and by segment
			• Customer bonding
			  – Switching costs
				• System market share
				• Our share of complementors
				  – % of investments tied to our proprietary standard
				• Our profit by complementor

(Continued).

Table 3.2. (*Continued*).

	Strategic Positioning		
	Best product	**Total customer solutions**	**System lock-in**

Innovation (renewal drivers)	• Rate of product introduction
	• Time to market
	• Percent of sales from new products
	• Cost of product development
	• R&D as % of sales
		• Relative involvement in customer value chain
		• Percent of product development
		  – From joint development
		  – Customized
		• Degree of product scope
		  (a) Current vs. potential bundling
			• Switching costs for complementors and for customers
			• Rate of product development
			• Cost of competitors to imitate standard

Source: Hax and Wilde (2001).

The over-riding purpose of competitive strategies is their ability to secure long-term financial value. These two are linked primarily through:

- The net operating cash flow margin
- Fixed and working capital investment, less divestment
- The economies of scale (which depend on the proportion of variable to fixed costs)
- The volume of sales to be generated
- The duration of that volume
- The offering's cost of capital

Each element and anticipated result of competitive strategy is then examined for its effect on these following financial variables. However, like the previous authors, they do not attempt in anyway to quantify their impact.

The work by Bromwich and Bhimani (1991) was the only one we are aware of, which tried specifically to incorporate strategy considerations into an augmented financial analysis framework. For this they proposed a framework that explicitly considers strategic benefits which can be derived from investments, both within the company and externally in its market positioning:

1. Internal strategies

    - Cost advantages
    - More control of production systems
    - Improved organisation
    - Beneficial interactions

2. Market strategies

    - **Diversification** — Expanded product portfolio, New products with new skills, New skills in new areas
    - **Enhancement** of existing products — Enhanced corporate image, Response to fluctuating demand, Lower cost of meeting demand, Improved quality
    - **Risk Reduction** — Stronger skill base, Better control and planning, Reduced working capital, More flexible responses)

In the end, they explicitly blended the financial quantification and qualitative strategic analysis in a normalised scale.

Reflection on Learnings

"What three (or four) lessons have we learned?"

1. Conventional financial analysis has major weaknesses when applied to major investments in technological change:

   - mis-assessment of the appropriate weighted average cost of capital and discount rate
   - undue optimism in projecting continuing stable returns
   - inability to account for "intangible" versus "tangible" benefits

2. Financial project evaluation metrics often ignore or fail to capture key considerations in business strategy, leading to a mismatch between strategic planning and actual operations. This arises from the inability of conventional techniques (based on discounted cash flow) to capture qualitative issues such as flexibility and externalities whose complexity, indirect impact and uncertainty makes them difficult to incorporate into financial measures.

3. Numerous schemes have been offered to complement traditional finance-oriented corporate decision-making. Insights from these schemes can be used to clarify the indirect, intangible, and hard-to-measure sources of value in a project, and ensure a 'strategic fit'.

"How do I put them into practical application?"

A. Strategic considerations not only impact future cash flows, but more specifically, impact the *planning period*, or the duration over which positive cash flows are generated.

B. While financial analysis might calculate the magnitude of income and point out the need to reduce product and capital costs or increase revenues, strategic analysis is necessary to calculate the duration of that income.

C. A three-step process can be used to link customer value to shareholder value:

   - Determine how well you currently meet the customer's shifting price, product and non-product needs (diagnosis)

- Build precision strategies that do a superior job of meeting these needs profitably (bridge)
- Make sure the strategies create enough customer and shareholder value to make them work (payoff).

4

A WAY FORWARD: QUANTITATIVE DECISION MAKING MEASURES

The Enhanced NPV

With the basic definition of the NPV, one introduces the time-value of money by comparing with the standard cost of capital, assumed to be constant with time, comparing the return of the investment with the risk-free return, defined as that of a US 90 days bonds. Otherwise, the cost of capital can be calculated with a weighted average according to the standard financial Weighted Average Cost of Capital formulation. However, in these two cases one assumes that the cost of capital is *constant* in time, which is not necessarily true. In particular, in a project evaluation scenario, one needs to include the idea of time-pressure. A project giving higher returns in the short term should be promoted over one giving long term returns. Even if two projects give the same overall NPV, one needs to promote the one that provides faster returns.

Uncertainty concept

This need is driven by the widely accepted notion of uncertainty in the return forecasts. This is the basic principle of the unpredictability of the forecasts; therefore, the shorter the return time, the more accurate the prediction. In the parallel field of finance, this belief is the cornerstone of the description of price dynamics as a random process. Since the 1980s, it has been recognised in the physical sciences that the unpredictable time series and random processes are quite similar. Wiener made the mathematics of the process describing the random motion of a speck of dust suspended in the air so rigorous that now the same concept and method has spread across almost all research areas in the natural sciences. In 1900, Bachelier determined the probability of price changes, in the financial market, as a Wiener process which satisfies the diffusion equation. Einstein rediscovered this point in 1905 in his paper on Brownian motion (the same motion of a speck of dust...). The problems of spreading a solute in a solvent can be cast in a similar equation, and solved in the same way. The Black & Scholes model to calculate the value of stock options is based on the "diffusion" equation of the logarithm of the prices in the financial market, and it is solved in the same way. It would be suggestive to apply the same concepts to the uncertainly of future cash flow in the NPV calculation...

The model

We propose that the NPV of future cash flow should be changed, and be a better representative of the fact that a quick return is more valuable than a long-term return. This is already captured in some way in the usual calculation of the NPV. Here we are proposing a mathematical model that enhances this concept. The Enhanced NPV should be represented according to a law inspired by the diffusion equation:

$$PV^* = R \exp(-bt^2),$$

where R is the expected return. This expression can be rewritten for a discrete time variable — the more usual accounting of time in terms of days, months or years — as:

$$PV^* = \frac{R}{(1+h)^{t^2}}.$$

Where the 'continuous time' discount rate b is linked to the 'discrete time' rate h:

$$b = ln(1+h), \quad \text{or} \quad h = e^b - 1.$$

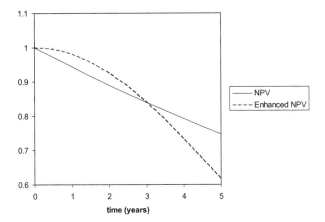

Figure 4.1. Plot of the — NPV discounting factor, compared to the — Enhanced NPV discounting factor.

By plotting this function, it is clear that the enhanced NPV, or PV*, curve lies above the traditional NPV curve only for some initial time t^*; after that time the two curves cross, and the enhanced NPV falls below the traditional NPV calculation. This feature it rather appealing for our purpose, since it promotes forecasts with quick high returns, over forecasts where high returns are expected at later times. Setting the cross over time is rather arbitrary. If this calculation is to be used in project evaluation, with fast returns desirable over a three-year period, the cross over at year three folds out naturally. With this constraint, the relation between the discount rate k in traditional NPV calculation is related to h via:

$$h = \exp\{3/9 \ln(1 + k)\} - 1.$$

The Capital Scale Index

The issue with the traditional Acid Test (AT), or the ratio between the total capital spend over the total return, is that it is a relative measure. Two business units, A and B, could agree in a partnership based on the same AT, for sharing the same risk. This concept is very well known in the economics literature, on how (relative and absolute) risk aversion varies with wealth and/or other circumstances.

In fact, they could have invested quite different capitals; therefore, the capital risk for the two entities is quite different. For example, let us consider business unit A investing $I = 100$ with an anticipated return of $R = 20$, sharing the same investment with business unit B with common Acid Test value: $AT = I/R = 100/20 = 5$. On the other hand business unit B has invested $I = 1000$ with an expected return of $R = 200$. Even if the Acid Test is the same, the capital involved is highly skewed. Of course business B is bearing a higher capital risk.

Scale issues

In financial indexing, one is always tempted to consider a constant cost of capital k, but in reality, the cost of capital must depend on the amount of capital involved. Higher capital involvement should lead to higher risk, and higher expected returns. Therefore, the linear function I/R proposed by the Acid Test calculation falls short in this respect.

The model

We address this issue by proposing simple analytical forms to keep track of the magnitude of the capital invested, which is stronger than linear. In principle, one can choose among an infinite set of functional forms, from power law to exponential. We opt for the analytical function that is the slowest growing, such as the logarithm. The logarithm, base 10, is also linked to the order or magnitude of the capital involved. Therefore, it can provide an immediate feedback on the net amount of capital involved.

The model proposes to multiply the Acid Test by the logarithm of the capital invested:

$$CSI = I \log(I)/R.$$

In the previous case the two business units will have

$$CSI(A) = 100 \times 2/20 = 10$$
$$CSI(B) = 1000 \times 3/200 = 15.$$

Clearly the capital scale index (CSI) test is higher for business unit B than for A.

A simple application example

As a simple application to exemplify the two quantities just introduced, let us consider two model projects, which are expected to produce a positive 5-year cash flow in conjunction with an initial one-time investment. These two projects have the same late-time return feature in the predicted cash flow, and are only different for the scale of the numbers involved. In the first analysis, we consider Cases 1a and 1b as described in Table 4.1, which share the same progression in the returns, the only difference being a different scale of the investment (and of the return). The numbers in Case 1b are exactly 10 times the numbers used in Case 1a.

Note that the two cases share the same Discounted Cash Flow yield, but are clearly differentiated by the NPV, which increases by an order of magnitude in the Case 1b, as one would expect. Even the usual Acid Test calculation fails in differentiating between the two scenarios, giving the same value of 0.91 for both. The proposed Capital Scale index ratio

Table 4.1. Summary of the Cash Flow and financial measures for projects (1a) and (1b), which are representative of a late return example.

Figures in €'000

Years	0 year 1	1 year 2	2 year 3	3 year 4	4 year 5	5 year 6
(1a) Net Cash Flow in constant terms	(100)	5	10	20	40	80
6.00% NPV factors	1.000000	0.943396	0.889996	0.839619	0.792094	0.747258
1.96% Enh NPV factors	1.000000	0.980764	0.925249	0.839619	0.732883	0.615343

Indicators	Sum	Acid Test	Capital Scale Index			
REVENUES	155	0.65	1.29			
NPV REVENUES	122	0.82	1.64			
Enhanced NPV REVENUES	109	0.91	1.83			
D.C.F. YIELD	11.3%					
Payback (n. years)	4.3					
NET PRESENT VALUE	22					
ENHANCED NPV	9					

(1b) Net Cash Flow in constant terms	(1,000)	50	100	200	400	800
6.00% NPV factors	1.000000	0.943396	0.889996	0.839619	0.792094	0.747258
1.96% Enh NPV factors	1.000000	0.980764	0.925249	0.839619	0.732883	0.615343

Indicators	Sum	Acid Test	Capital Scale Index			
TOTAL REVENUES	1,550	0.65	1.94			
NPV REVENUES	1,219	0.82	2.46			
Enhanced NPV REVENUES	1,095	0.91	2.74			
D.C.F. YIELD	11.3%					
Payback (n. years)	4.3					
NET PRESENT VALUE	219					
ENHANCED NPV	95					

Table 4.2. Summary of the Cash Flow and financial measures for projects (2a) and (2b), which are representative of a fast return example.

Figures in €'000

Years	0 year 1	1 year 2	2 year 3	3 year 4	4 year 5	5 year 6
(2a) Net Cash Flow in constant terms	(100)	80	40	20	10	5
6.00% NPV factors	1.000000	0.943396	0.889996	0.839619	0.792094	0.747258
1.96% Enh NPV factors	1.000000	0.980764	0.925249	0.839619	0.732883	0.615343

Indicators	Sum	Acid Test	Capital Scale Index			
TOTAL REVENUES	155	0.65	1.29			
NPV REVENUES	140	0.72	1.43			
Enhanced NPV REVENUES	143	0.70	1.40			
D.C.F. YIELD	29.3%					
Payback (n. years)	1.5					
NET PRESENT VALUE	40					
ENHANCED NPV	43					

	0 year 1	1 year 2	2 year 3	3 year 4	4 year 5	5 year 6
(2b) Net Cash Flow in constant terms	(1,000)	800	400	200	100	50
6.00% NPV factors	1.000000	0.943396	0.889996	0.839619	0.792094	0.747258
1.96% Enh NPV factors	1.000000	0.980764	0.925249	0.839619	0.732883	0.615343

Indicators	Sum	Acid Test	Capital Risk Index			
TOTAL REVENUES	1,550	0.65	1.94			
NPV REVENUES	1,395	0.72	2.15			
Enhanced NPV REVENUES	1,427	0.70	2.10			
D.C.F. YIELD	29.3%					
Payback (n. years)	1.5					
NET PRESENT VALUE	395					
ENHANCED NPV	427					

still captures the difference in the scale of the capital involved, and jumps from 1.83 to 2.74, revealing that the 'capital risk' involved with the project described in Case 1a is smaller than that in Case 1b.

In the second example (see Table 4.2), we considered two projects (2a and 2b) in the same time-span of predicted cash flows, which represent fast-time return.

Here, again, the Capital Scale index increases going from 1.40 to 2.10 when the initial capital involved increases from 100 to 1000.

It is even more interesting to perform a cross comparison within Table 4.3. The total returns of Project 1a and 2a are the same (if we forget for the moment the time-value of money) yielding a total revenue of 155. The returns, though, are distributed in a different way along the time frame. Project 2a has a much faster rate of returns. This is readily indicated by the classical measure of the classical NPV, which jumps from 22 to 40 for fast returns. Here, Project 2a should be preferred by a factor almost 2

Table 4.3. Summary of current measures and proposed measures.

	Current Measures				Proposed Measures	
	NPV	DCF Yield	Payback	Acid Test	Enh NPV	CSI
Project (1a)	22	11.30%	4.5y	0.82	9	1.83
Project (2a)	40	29.30%	1.8y	0.72	43	1.4
ratio (2a)/(1a)	*1.8*	*2.6*	*0.4*	*0.9*	*4.8*	*0.8*

(40/22). The Enhanced NPV is much more sensitive to the rate of returns, promoting Project 2a by a factor near to 5 (43/9). This means that the comparison between the two Enhanced NPVs would be able to respond to even slight differences in the speed of the returns, and therefore, provide a better decision tool to promote fast returns projects.

The same concept is captured by the increase in traditional DCF yield: 11.3% versus 29.3% for the fast-returns project. According to this calculation, returns for Project 2a are 2.6 ($= 29.3/11.3$) times faster than for Project 1a. Similar results are obtained with the Payback calculation, which yields a factor 2.5 difference between the two projects. Let us reiterate the point on sensitivity: both DCF yield and Payback would pick up a factor 2.5 difference versus the factor 5 difference obtained by Enhanced NPV calculations.

One last comment on the cumulative measure of the Capital Scale index. The Capital Scale Index goes from 1.83 down to 1.40, indicating that Project 2a bears the lowest risk. A similar result could be achieved by using the classic Acid test calculation, yielding 0.82 and 0.70. Once again, the proposed new measure is more sensitive and would be able to pick up and enhance even the slightest variation in the risk involved in the capital invested up front or the speed of the rate of returns.

Of the four scenarios, the Capital Scale Index predicts that Project 2a is to be preferred, since it involves low capital investment up front and a fast rate of returns.

The Operating Value Added Model

This particular definition of economic value added is not different, in essence, from the residual income indicators outlined in the previous chapters, as it rests of the sum of three contributions: the discounted operating cash flow in the forecast period, plus the estimated marked value of the business at the end of the plan, minus the estimated current value of the business. As usual, we would like to start from the cash flow statement, and calculate the Operating Cash Flow (OCF) according to the standard financial definition:

$$F(t) = OCF_i(t).$$

Here, the operating cash flow OCF includes the profit from operating activities, depreciation, dividend not paid out, purchase of fixed assets, working capital movement and loan finance items.

The present value of cash flow is simply obtained by the standard discounting procedure:

$$F^{\otimes}(t) = \frac{F(t)}{(1+k)^t} = \frac{F_i(t) - F_0(t)}{(1+k)^t},$$

where k is the weighted average cost of capital. The definition above is the basis for capturing the differential value added — this is why we need to subtract the operating cash flow at time 0. The cumulative value of the discounted value of cash flow over the time window going from $\tau = 1$ to t is:

$$F_c^{\otimes}(t) = \sum_{\tau=1}^{t} F^{\otimes}(t).$$

Now let us calculate the current and terminal values of the business. In the standard procedure, these are calculated using a perpetuity model, where the operating cash flow is used as an estimate of the future continuous income. This leads directly to the definition of CV (Market Value), according to the perpetuity model:

$$CV = \sum_{0}^{\infty} \frac{F(0)}{(1+k)^t} = \frac{F(0)}{k}.$$

The Terminal Value (TV) is calculated in the same way, and its present value is calculated with the appropriate discounting procedure.

The combination of the three terms, discounted cumulative operating cash flow plus TV minus CV at the beginning of the forecast period, represent the OVA:

$$OVA = F_c^\otimes(t) + TV_t - CV_0.$$

Lifetime of the project

One shortcoming in this calculation is the assumption of constant OCF for a long (infinite) time, when one reasonably expects that the project will be profitable only within a reasonable time frame. The project is expected to produce a substantial, or non-negligible, operating cash flow, only within a time τ, which we shall call the 'profit time'. This time threshold may depend on many financial and business factors, which are the presence of external competitors, the loss of a market share, loss of consumer interest in the product or a change in the business strategy of the company.

It is not unreasonable to imagine that the operating cash flow, within the life cycle of the project will undergo a profitability cycle. Many functional forms can portray this cycle — and we have chosen, for mathematical simplicity, the functional form of a parabola. (Similar qualitative results are obtained with similar functional form). Again, we assume that the curve raises to a maximum of order twice the initial operating cash flow. This assumption is reasonable, if we neglect any active influence of the management to improve operating margins, or to push production, and that the market is not extremely positive or reactive.

One possible analytical function, which captures these financial concepts, is a parabolic profile of the OCF(t):

$$OCF(t) = OCF_0 \left(-\frac{8}{\tau^2}t^2 + \frac{8}{\tau}t \right)$$

which can be easily used in the calculation of the current value of the business, by going to the continuum limit of the sum:

$$CV = \sum_0^\tau \frac{OCF(t)}{(1+k)^t} = \int_0^\tau dt\, OCF(t)e^{-\bar{k}t}$$

$$= OCF_0 \frac{8\left(e^{-\bar{k}\tau}\bar{k}\tau + 2e^{-\bar{k}\tau} - 2 + \bar{k}\tau\right)}{\bar{k}^3\tau^2},$$

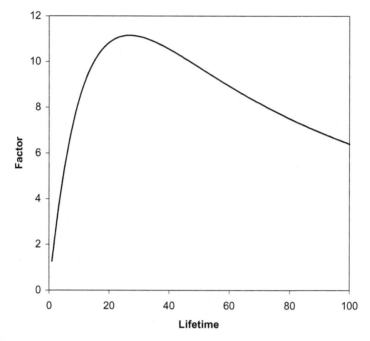

Figure 4.2. The rate-dependent factor of the model for CV plotted as a function of the business lifetime τ.

where the sum (and the integral) is extended only up to the 'profit time' τ, and $\bar{k}$ is the continuous discount rate corresponding to the discrete discount rate k ($\ln \bar{k} = 1 + k$). Notice that the CV is given by the initial OCF times a function of τ, and $\bar{k}$. This function reaches a maximum value of approximately $1/\bar{k}$ at $\tau \approx 25$ years, which is similar to the multiplicative result one would obtain using the perpetuity model, indicating that this extension is compatible with previous studies (Figure 4.2).

Real options

We have also noted in the previous chapters that conventional financial methods, using estimates of future cash flows, fail to place a numerical value on the choice, kept open by the project, to invest (or not to invest) in response to the behaviour of the market. Although management may be aware of this failure to place a monetary value on the flexibility provided by future choices, there would be a clear advantage to be had from any new financial approach which can properly value the options created or available to the project. A strong candidate for consideration is the theory of real options. In the following application example, we choose to work with discrete time, and imagine that action will be taken halfway down the time line of the forecast period. The management will be faced with two options, the option to grow or to shrink the size of the project. And action will be taken either way, according to the market situation.

We, therefore, introduce a 'decision-time' τ_d, which for sake of simplicity will be taken to be equal to half the forecast time τ_f. The operating cash flow is expected to be higher in the positive scenario, and lower in the negative one, with respect to the forecast for OCF. The cumulative present value of the OCF will be the result of the sum:

$$F^{\otimes}(t) = \sum_{0}^{\tau_d} \frac{OCF(t)}{(1+k)^t} + \begin{cases} \sum_{\tau_d}^{\tau_f} \frac{OCF_+(t)}{(1+k)^t} & \text{positive} \\[2mm] \sum_{\tau_d}^{\tau_f} \frac{OCF(t)}{(1+k)^t} & \text{neutral} \\[2mm] \sum_{\tau_d}^{\tau_f} \frac{OCF_-(t)}{(1+k)^t} & \text{negative} \end{cases},$$

where we have split the sum into two terms, the first ranging from time 0 to τ_d, and the second from τ_d to τ_f. Of course, a different course of action will involve different capitals involved. In the positive scenario, management will commit to an expansion of the project, following an additional investment to allow for the expansion of the production — the Investment for Growth (Ig). This quantity needs to be included in the total NPV calculation. In the negative marked environment, management might decide to downsize the operations, reducing effectively the operating cash flow, and securing an additional capital — the investment to 'shrink' (Is), following the disposal of part(s) of the fixed assets.

The growth option involves an analytical evaluation of the extended NPV. Here V represents the rightmost piece of the above summation in the different cases, and E the extended NPV:

$$E = pE^+ + (1-p)E^-,$$

Table 4.4. Hypothetical business situation involving historical data (years –5 to 0) and forecasted data (years 1–5).

Time	-5	-4	-3	-2	-1	0	1	2	3	4	5
Market Size (NPS)	33,980	34,999	36,049	37,131	38,245	39,392	40,574	41,791	43,045	44,336	45,666
Market Growth %	3%	3%	3%	3%	3%	3%	3%	3%	3%	3%	3%
Market Share	8.0%	8.1%	7.9%	8.0%	8.0%	8.1%	8.1%	8.2%	8.2%	8.3%	8.3%
Total revenue	2,730	2,821	2,865	2,968	3,075	3,185	3,301	3,420	3,542	3,670	3,801
Gross profit	**210**	**217**	**224**	**234.5**	**245**	**255.5**	**267.75**	**280**	**292.25**	**306.25**	**318.5**
Fixed Assets	735	754	774	802	830	861	893	922	956	991	1,015
Working Capital	263	275	287	298	308	320	333	341	354	368	380
Total Capital Employed	**998**	**1,029**	**1,061**	**1,099**	**1,138**	**1,181**	**1,225**	**1,264**	**1,309**	**1,358**	**1,395**

where

$$E^+ = \max(V^+, V^+ - \text{Ig})$$
$$E^- = \max(V^-, V^- - \text{Ig}),$$

and p is the probability of this scenario to be realised. This number should be calculated rigorously from a market-related variable, but can also be reasonably estimated at the time of the forecast.

The shrink option evaluation is quite similar in the analytical form of the extended NPV:

$$E = pE^+ + (1 - p)E^-,$$

where

$$E^+ = \max(V^+, V^+ + \text{Is})$$
$$E^- = \max(V^-, V^- + \text{Is}),$$

and p is the probability of this scenario to be realised.

An application example

The financial data of a hypothetical business scenario are shown in Table 4.4, where the time index ranges from year −5 to year 5. Data relative to year −5 to year 0 represent historical figures, whereas data relative to year 1 to year 5 are forecasted. We have applied the financial indicators only to the forecasted period. This example is also enriched with a management decision option at year 3, as it is explained in Figure 4.3. At that time, management will revise the behaviour of the market, and has two options. Essentially the management has to decide whether to invest more in the business and increase the operating cash flow by 10% or to reduce

---

Real option In year 3, the management has to take a decision whether to either expand or reduce the business activity. The expansion or reduction decision will increase or decrease, respectively, the Cash Flow in the measure of 10%. Also the additional investment to go either way is equal to 10% of the Total capital employed at year 3, i.e. 74.8. Finally, the probability that the management will decide to expand the business is 40%, whereas the probability to reduce the activity is 60%.

Figure 4.3. An important management decision (real option) has to be taken at the beginning of year 3. The result will affect the future business revenues.

Table 4.5. The financial indicators necessary to calculate the business value according to the different evaluation approaches are reported in the table.

Time	-5	-4	-3	-2	-1	0	1	2	3	4	5
Rappaport											
Flow in	132	137	141	148	154	161	169	176	184	193	201
Flow out		32	32	39	39	44	44	39	46	49	37
Cash Flow		105	110	109	116	117	125	138	139	144	164
SV		3,009	3,065	3,153	3,236	3,309	3,396	3,483	3,560	3,644	3,719
Stewart											
Flow in	132	137	141	148	154	161	169	176	184	193	201
Flow out	60	62	64	66	68	71	74	76	79	81	84
Cash Flow	72	75	77	82	86	90	95	101	106	111	117
EVA	72	75	77	82	86	90	95	101	106	111	117
MVA	97	192	284	376	467	557	647	736	825	913	1,001
Operating Cash Flow	106	111	115	120	127	135	135	142	152	158	160

the business activity, and thus the operating cash flow by 10%, by paying a redundancy package, etc.

In Table 4.5, we look into the details of the calculation of the financial indicators, as they are based on different calculation of the cash flow. Notice that SVA and OVA definitions of the cash flow are very close to each other, while the cash flow estimated in EVA differs quite markedly from the first two. Table 4.6 summarises the relevant contributions to the calculation of the financial indicators, namely the current value, terminal value and the forecast plan value, for the three different approaches and the Total Business Return.

The first part of Table 4.6 shows how the elements of the business case of Table 4.4 are evaluated under the traditional approaches and OVA. In particular, the current and terminal values of the business determined under SVA and OVA are quite similar as their calculation is based on similar financial elements: the forecast of the future sales for SVA and the forecast of the future operating cash flow for EVA.

On the contrary, within the EVA model, the current value of the business is estimated by adding up the value of EVA from the start of the business

Table 4.6. Comparison table for the studied financial indicators. For the sake of completeness Total Business Return evaluation (TBR) is also added to the table. The first part of the table corresponds to the classic calculation of the operators without any additional consideration for the lifetime of the business and the occurrence of a real option. The second part of the table collects the revised calculation of CV and TV when a lifetime for the business is taken into account. The third part of the table shows the numerical impact of real options (management response to market change) on the calculation of the value added.

Indicators	EVA	SVA	TBR	OVA
Classic				
Current Value	557	2,683	2,156	2,244
Plan Value	444	593	643	625
Terminal Value	748	2,499	1,924	1,992
Value Added	634	**410**	411	**374**
Time (business' life)				
Current Value			640	640
Plan Value			625	625
Terminal Value			568	568
Value Added			**554**	**554**
Real Options				
Value Added			**576**	**576**

until the year to date. In our case, the sum runs from year –5 to year 0. We notice the same trends when comparing the plan value of the business in the three different approaches. SVA, EVA and OVA use the same NPV approach to calculate that figure, however, the cash flow value used in EVA is different than the one used in SVA and EVA. In summary, all the approaches evaluate the business activity of Table 4.4 as positive and having similar value added.

The second part of the table in Table 4.6 shows the impact of the business lifetime when calculating the initial and terminal value of the business itself. This is especially important when evaluating a business where the profitability is strongly time-dependent, as is the case the new economy. One can safely assume that the business will be profitable in a short time frame (*e.g.* 3–5 years); therefore, the CV estimate should assume positive cash flow only for a limited time. This is in contrast with the traditional perpetuity model, where the cash flow is assumed to be constant for all the years to come from now to infinity. Of course no change affects the calculation of the plan value. Because of the assumption of short profitability time, and parabolic behaviour of the projected cash flows, the current and terminal values of the business are lower than the values calculated when following the classic approach (perpetuity model). As a consequence, the numerical value of the forecast period plays a more relevant part in the evaluation of the business value added.

Finally, in the third part of the table of Table 4.6, the value added by the business activity is reported when taking into account the option available to the management to increase or decrease the business activity at the third year. As we expected, the value added (576) is higher than the value calculated in previous section (554) reflecting the fact that management response to change in the market parameters adds value to the business.

In the research study, the robustness of the proposed enhancement have been tested to ensure that were performing in line with the expectations and field experience evidences on the ground of key drivers . The results of the test can be found in the Appendix.

Reflection on Learnings

"What three (or four) lessons have we learned?"

1. In classical NPV calculations, it is assumed that the cost of capital is *constant* in time, which is not essentially true. In particular, in a project evaluation scenario, one needs to include the idea of time-pressure. A project giving higher returns in the short-term should be promoted over one giving long term returns. Even if two projects give the same overall NPV, one needs to promote the one that provides faster returns. This is the basic principle of the unpredictability of the forecasts; therefore, the shorter the return time, the more accurate the prediction.

2. In financial indexing, one is always tempted to consider a constant cost of capital k, but in reality the cost of capital must depend on the amount of capital involved. Higher capital involvement should lead to higher risk, and higher expected returns. Therefore, the linear function I/R proposed by the Acid Test calculation falls short in this respect.

3. One shortcoming in the estimate of the CV or the TV, is the assumption of constant Cash Flow for a long (infinite) time, whereas one reasonably expects that the project will be profitable only within a reasonable time frame. The project is expected to produce a substantial, or non-negligible, operating cash flow, only within a time t, which we shall call the 'profit time'. This time threshold may depend on many financial and business factors, which are the presence of external competitors, the loss of a market share, loss of consumer interest in the product, or a change in the business strategy of the company.

4. Conventional financial methods, using estimates of future cash flows, fail to place a numerical value on the choice, kept open by the project, to invest (or not to invest) later in response to the behaviour of the market. Although management may be aware of this failure to place a monetary value on the flexibility provided by future choices, there would be a clear advantage to be had from any new financial approach which can properly value the options created or available to the project.

"How do I put them into practical application?"

A. We propose that the NPV of future cash flow should be changed, and be a better representation of the fact that a quick return is more valuable

73

than a long-term return:

$$PV^* = R/(1+k)^{t2}$$

where R is the return at year t, and k is the cost of capital.

B. We propose simple analytical forms to take into account the magnitude of the capital invested over the cost of capital, which is stronger than linear. The Capital Scale Index (CSI) proposes to multiply the Acid Test (AT) by the logarithm of the capital invested:

$$\text{CSI} = \frac{I}{R} \log I$$

C. It is not unreasonable to imagine that the operating cash flow, within the life cycle of the project will undergo a profitability parabola. One possible analytical function, which captures this financial concept, is a parabolic profile, which rises to a maximum after a certain time, and then drops to 0 at the end of the business cycle.

D. We propose the method of 'real options' to assign a numerical value to management flexibility: this quantifies the value of the option to grow or to downsize a business or a project. This formalism is derived from the techniques used to estimate the value of stock options.

5

A WAY FORWARD: QUALITATIVE
DECISION MAKING MEASURES

Project Value Chain

This framework is the starting point for the strategic analysis, and is based
on Porter's Project Value Chain (Porter, 1980). Two series of drivers would
be able to influence this value chain; some of them are key to enhance
value (promote higher turnover and growth), and some are the trigger for
enhanced profits (reduce all types of costs).

Value enablers

Among the listed value enablers, several are generally recognised in the literature as those readily expandable by complementary suppliers. We identify specific supply chain drivers for each of these.

Innovation/new technology

The willingness of suppliers to cheaply make complementary adjustments
corresponding to the development of new technologies plays a direct role
in determining the extent to which a company can leverage its intellectual
property and the pace of technology evolution in a company's offerings.
This is particularly true in the case when suppliers contribute a good deal
of the final product architecture, when suppliers are closely integrated into

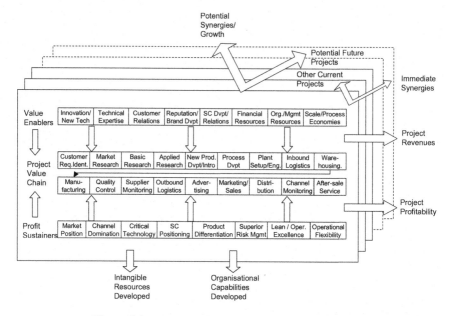

Figure 5.1. Framework for project value chain analysis.

the production process, or where the pace of innovation is fast. In many cases, suppliers may be the first to come into contact with new technologies through their business in other industries.

Technical expertise

The willingness of suppliers to share production experience, adjust production schedules and processes, and otherwise provide process feedback will affect the speed and the extent of learning achievable downstream.

Customer relations

The willingness of suppliers to engage and adjust to downstream customer demands can complement the company's own marketing efforts. This is particularly true when the supplier provides complementary downstream activities, such as parts servicing, channel monitoring or distribution, in addition to typical supply relations to the company.

Supply chain development/relations

In nearly all instances of Supply Chain Management best practices, co-operation between a company and its suppliers involves a two-way exchange of good faith, usually promoted by long-term incentive contracts and alliances.

Financial resources

Many companies have required suppliers to share development costs, absorb inventory fluctuations, assume operating, currency risk and guarantee fixed costs or continuous cost reduction. This frees up financial resources and reduced the company's exposure to project risk.

Profit sustainers

Although all of the profit sustainers can be influenced by suppliers to some degree, the following five are most significantly affected.

Supply chain positioning

Winning critical partners in the supply network, whether through alliances or long-term contracts, can yield access to critical resources and markets. Where these arrangements are exclusive and involve a critical technology or market, a first-mover can achieve monopolistic market positions and channel domination. Developing viable second-sourcing options can also strengthen the bargaining power of companies vis-à-vis suppliers. Positioning the company in natural convergence or nodal points on the supply chain may also yield coordination rents.

Product differentiation

Suppliers play a critical role in product differentiation when attractive features they provide are incorporated into a company's existing offerings and packages. Supplier co-operation is essential in performing this in an efficient and creative manner.

Superior risk management

In addition to the benefits provided by drawing on the suppliers' financial strength discussed earlier, closer relationships and frequent feedback with suppliers can often provide improved situational awareness and early warning of potential problems. Early involvement of suppliers in the risk evaluation process itself can also broaden a company's experience base.

Lean/operational excellence

Operational goals such as just-in-time delivery, customer pull, zero defects are all impossible with total supply chain involvement and commitment.

Operational flexibility

A broad supply base operating efficient markets can contribute greatly to operational flexibility, particularly in products with highly variable demand and when the supplied component has application in a wide range of industries (*i.e.*, is low in industry specificity).

The Growth Matrix

The growth matrix is essentially one index, which captures all the non-financial (strategic) sources of value growth within a prospective project. By value we would mean "stakeholder value", which includes both customer value and profits for all supply chain participants.

We identified the value of a project to be based on two major elements:

Operational Value:

- *Revenues* and *profits* — financial analysis of project cash flows,
- *Operational effectiveness* — evaluates how the project helps achieve operational requirements not reflected in financial figures,
- *Operational efficiency* — Evaluate the ability in achieving continuous improvement above financial results and operational effectiveness, in the most favourable way,
- *Operational externalities* — evaluates immediate synergies vis-à-vis other and existing projects.

Business Value:

- *Resource accumulation* — evaluates resources accumulated, which may yield potential rents on this and future projects,
- *Capability development* — evaluates capabilities developed which may impact future projects,
- *Industry structure/conduct* — evaluates impact on industry structure and the level of competition within the industry and
- *Business characteristics* — evaluates impact on the way business is conducted, key operating characteristics, and order-qualifying/-winning criteria within the industry.

In evaluating a project, what we need then is a tightly integrated framework simultaneously examining these sources of value in the context of organisational, technological, and business issues in key business processes within the value chain, namely product development and product delivery, as well as key linkages with the customer and supply chain.

We have constructed two matrices, the *operational growth matrix* and *business growth matrix*, based on the above distinction (Table 5.1). The relative importance and content of each of these matrices depends on unique set of circumstances facing each project and the company's involved.

In principle this is the complete matrix that should be considered when evaluating growth both from the operational and the business point of view. In project evaluation, it would be difficult, and probably not important to perform an exhaustive analysis. Most often the company strategy is focussed on some of the elements outlined in the more general matrix. The company typically defines some **critical success factors**, which would be met if some of the elements of the matrix were met to a certain degree. Each strategy may devise specific measures or project evaluation tools, which capture one or more of these categories. We have prepared a sample project evaluation questionnaire based on these matrices.

Example of operational growth questionnaire

1. Product development

    a. How well does this project employ integrated product and process design and integrated product teams to maximise available

Table 5.1. The operational and business growth matrices.

Strategic Project Evaluation		Operational Growth Matrix		
		Operational Effectiveness	Operational Efficiency	Operational Externalities
Processes	Product Development	Does the product development pipeline offer the right products at the right time?	Are the product development process optimised for lead-time, cost, etc.	Makes development of other products more effective or efficient?
Processes	Product Delivery	Provide competive cost, dependability, flexibility, quality and speed? Achieve continuous product/process improvement?	Actively eliminate waste? Pursue lean? Achieve continuous cost reduction?	Makes delivery of other products more efffective or efficient?
Linkages	Customer Involvement	Does the project maximise customer interaction and responsiveness?	Are mechanisms for customer interaction optimally coordinated?	Facilitates customer involvement on other projects?
Linkages	Supply Chain Management	Does the project promote supply chain management best practices? Will suppliers be able to contribute significant additional value?	Are suppliers best practices, monitoring, and involvement optimally coordinated?	Facilitates supply chain management on other projects?

Strategic Project Evaluation		Business Growth Matrix			
		Resource Accumulation	Capability Development	Industry Structure/Conduct	Business Characteristics
Processes	Product Development	Acquire/develop useful product development resources?	Build and refine new or existing product development capabilities?	Can improved product development processes alter industry structure or level of competition?	Fundamentally alter product characteristics (usage, content, technology, etc)?
Processes	Product Delivery	Acquire/develop useful product delivery resources?	Build and refine new or existing product delivery capabilities?	Can improved product delivery process alter industry structure or level of competition?	Fundamentally alter product delivery processes (channels, production techniques, logistics, etc)?
Linkages	Customer Involvement	Acquire/develop resources for effective customer involvement (i.e. power, trust, IT, data, habits, image)	Develop or improve channels/mechanisms or customer interaction?	Does customer involvement promote a more favourable industry structure or reduce competition?	Fundamentally alter nature of customers interaction ith the product and the firm?
Linkages	Supply Chain Management	Acquire/develop resources for effective supply chain mgmt (i.e. personnel, IPTs, IT, trust, power)	Develop or improve channels /mechanisms /routines for supply chain management?	Do supply chain proctices promote a more favourable industry structure or reduce competition?	Fundamentally alter nature of supplier roles on the project and with the firm?

information in addressing technology choice, manufacturability, marketability and other development issues?

b. How well does this project employ modularity and platform architecture in development to ensure maximum flexibility?

c. How well does this project employ concurrent engineering to reduce time-to-market?

2. Product delivery

   a. How much does this project allow for continuous product improvement and updating?

   b. Does this project outsource for the right reasons (customer value, technical know-how, market expertise, capacity flexibility, risk sharing, lead-time reduction, continuous cost-reduction, etc.)?

   c. Will this project be able to consistently offer the highest quality and reliability in the related market segment?

3. Customer requirements

   a. How much does this project improve our ability to understand market requirements and acquire customer feedback?

   b. How much does this project generate more customer participation and interaction during product development and delivery?

   c. How much does this project provide flexible customisation with fast response?

4. Supply chain

   a. How much will this project develop new strategic long-term partners or enhance our relationship with existing ones?

   b. How much does this project promote best practices among our suppliers?

Example of business growth questionnaire

1. Product development

   a. Does this project reinforce our leading brands?

   b. Does this project extend our product logic and modular platform strategy?

   c. Does this project improve our existing product innovation capability?

   d. Does this project acquire or develop significant product technology or intellectual property?

2. Product delivery

   a. Does this project improve our existing process innovation capability?

   b. Does this project acquire new process innovations (technologies, techniques, IT, etc.)?

    c. Does this project extend our strategy of continuous workforce improvement?

3. Customer involvement

    a. Does this project build on our regional market expertise?

    b. Does this project reinforce the market leadership of our existing product lines?

    c. How much does this project preserve or enhance brand, reputation and customer loyalty?

4. Supply chain management

    a. Will does this project acquire or develop key material/resource/location access necessary for effective future operations?

    b. How much will this project increase our influence and power over our suppliers in future projects?

    c. Can supplier arrangements for this project reduce the level of competition we face in this product segment?

Questionnaire data processing

Through the questionnaires, one can proceed and score the different elements, which capture the selected strategic thrusts. Scores for example could be given in a scale from 0–5 for each question, on the basis of each cluster of elements. Of course the scoring criteria should be comparable within the cluster, as it is a relative quantity, but not across different categories. The results should be properly weighted according to the relative importance that the strategy into action has assigned to specific areas. We suggest the development of a 'filtering mask', shown in Table 5.2. The relative weights, 1–7, have to be decided at the strategic level, with the attempt to give a mathematical support to the prioritisation of the strategy into action. Of course this strategy is bound to change as time goes by.

Therefore this 'filter mask' should be updated when the priorities have changed, and the organisation is pushing towards a different growth paradigm. The resulting weighted scores, indicated in Table 5.2, are then

Table 5.2. Example of scores of the Operational Growth questionnaire.

Operational Growth	Score [0–5]	Mask [1–7]	Impact	
Product development				10
Integration	5	2	10	
Modularity	5	1	5	
Time-to-Market	5	3	15	
Product delivery				20
Improvement	5	5	25	
Outsource	5	6	30	
Quality/Reliability	5	1	5	
Customer requirements				13
Understanding	5	1	5	
Participation	5	4	20	
Flexibility	5	3	15	
Supply chain				13
Partnership	5	2	10	
Best Practice	5	3	15	
Growth indicator (sum)			**155**	
Growth indicator (avg)				**14**

analysed and the results are better viewed in a radar type plot. In the following example the numbers are assigned in a random matter, and have not been drawn from an actual project evaluation.

These two graphs report the maximum value that can be obtained, following the scoring of the matrix. Remember that we have used in this example a maximum (5) for each item, and weighted it according to the strategy mask. On the other hand, a less than perfect scoring in each item, will lead to shorter bars or a smaller area in Figure 5.2. This is a graphical representation of a gap analysis.

A similar argument goes for the graphical representation of the Business Growth questionnaire.

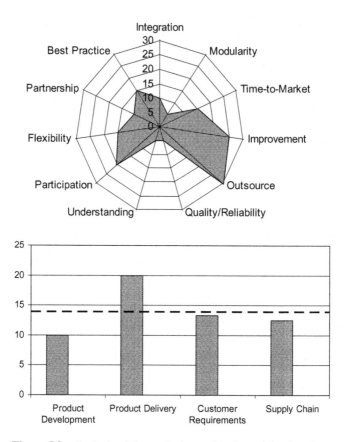

Figure 5.2. Analysis of the results in a radar plot and in a bar chart.

Risk Analysis

In the following sections, we address another aspect of project evaluation which is typically a blind-spot of traditional financial measures. This includes an evaluation of any possible occurrence of an event, which could affect (positively or negatively) the achievement of the objectives of the project.

Not even the Roman Sybil and the Greek Pythia can predict the future, but you can plan and try to anticipate what will happen. The plan will consist of a linked set of events, which are thought to be the most likely to occur. Normally everything should go according to the plan, however, sometimes events may occur, which you may not have made arrangements

Table 5.3. Example of scores of the Business Growth questionnaire.

Business growth	Score [0–5]	Mask [1-7]	Impact	
Product development				**9**
Leading brands	5	2	10	
Product logic	5	1	5	
Product capability	5	3	15	
Intellectual property	5	1	5	
Product delivery				**20**
Process capability	5	5	25	
Process innovation	5	6	30	
Workforce improvements	5	1	5	
Customer requirements				**13**
Multi-local multinational	5	1	5	
Market leadership	5	4	20	
Brand reputation	5	3	15	
Supply chain				**13**
Future operations	5	2	10	
Suppliers relationship	5	3	15	
Level of competition	5	3	15	
Growth indicator (sum)			**175**	
Growth indicator (avg)				**14**

for or may not have even considered. In your personal life, this can be dealt with by taking out an insurance policy. Such an action would financially compensate you, should an unwanted event occur. An example of this may be the unfortunate event that you need emergency repairs to your home or the accidental damage, fire, theft or malicious damage to your own car, or any damage you cause to other people and their property.

Risks permeate business. Risk is high in the agenda of decision-makers and spans across several areas, with significant impact on:

- Strategic planning
- Tactical planning
- Operational control/management

As discussed in the previous chapters, sound business decisions need a paradigm shift in the minds of the manager. Decision-making cannot be

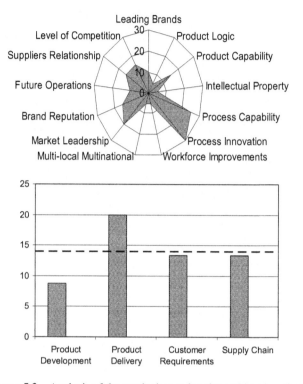

Figure 5.3. Analysis of the results in a radar plot and in a bar chart.

focused only on the best

- Maximum return/profit
- Minimum cost
- Shortest time of completion

In supporting decision making under uncertain conditions, the business manager needs to take into account the minimum risk, according to their own risk-tolerance. All risks must be identified and assessed to ensure that they do not adversely affect the business decisions. They must be planned for and controlled. This anticipation and planning is at the heart of taking decisions in uncertain conditions.

Definition of risk

Risk is the combination of three components (BS 4778 definition): "a combination of the probability or frequency of occurrence of a defined hazard and the magnitude of the consequences of the occurrence". These are:

- Impact: a measure of the magnitude of event outcome (= severity)
- Probability: probability of detrimental effect given the event occurs (= expectancy)
- Frequency: the frequency, that is, how often the risk event occurs

Risk can therefore be defined as a function of these components:

$$\text{Risk} = f(\text{impact, probability, frequency}).$$

Risk management

A proper account and management of risk includes identifying, analysing, and responding to that risk. It includes maximising the results of positive events (upside) and minimising the consequences of adverse events (downside). Most frequently, the business or decision maker relies (a) on his/her own judgement, (b) on experience of similar situations, and (c) on tools specifically developed for such a situation.

The final decision may be linked to the risk tolerance (linked to the relevant risk profile) of the decision maker. However, proper Risk Management is a proactive rather than a reactive process. In other words, it requires anticipation rather than reaction. When any project begins, the levels of tolerances must be understood from the outset and laid down in the risk management plan. Normally these are a corporate requirement, but they are also good practice in any business decision.

Risk management methodology

Risk management is a continuous and developing process and should address all risks that could affect an organisation in terms of timing and source (internal or external). It starts as a strategy when the project is being established and continues during the life cycle of a project until it is completed. Risk management includes several processes that, although shown as discrete elements here, are highly inter-related. These are:

- **Strategic Objectives:** Present the objectives we need to pursue and the impact we want to make on the market.
- **Identification**: Determine which risks are likely to affect the project and documenting the characteristics of each.
- **Quantification:** Evaluate the probability and consequences of risks and risk interactions on the possible range of outcomes to a project so as to examine and develop alternative options.
- **Mitigation:** Use techniques and methods for the reduction and control of risks or the enhancement of opportunities.
- **Control:** Document the lessons learned for future benefit.

Strategic objectives

The first phase of risk management is to understand the business strategy in terms of the objectives that we need to pursue, and the impact we want to make on the market.

Then the relevant strategy should tell us how we can leverage the internal and external components or constraints to achieve our objectives

Risk identification

The second phase of risk management is to identify and classify all the probable areas of risk. Their likelihood or importance should not be considered at the first stage, as these will be assessed at a later stage. Any source of information that allows for the recognition of a potential problem can be used for risk identification. A number of ways to identify risks are routinely in use, and have been reviewed elsewhere. Further methods for identifying risks include looking at the viewpoints of different people *e.g.* the customer. Examining customer requirements and desires may highlight some further risks.

There are numerous ways to classify risks in a business.

Table 5.4. Financial and non-financial risks.

Financial (Loss of Money)	Non Financial (Loss of life or limb)
• Market risk	• Environmental risk
• Credit risk	• Health, food & agriculture
• Liquidity risk	• Legal risk
• Foreign exchange risk	• Disasters (fire, earthquake, etc.)
	• Hostile activities and war
Project risk	
Corporate risk	

Here, we follow one of the possible classifications, which has been articulated by Gautam Mitra (Mitra, 2003). One of the most basic approaches is to divide everything up into two categories, such as financial and non-financial risks. The financial risks contain any type of opportunity for a profit or a loss, such as investing in a new product line, which may, at the end of the day, either sell well and make a profit for the company or not sell at all and have cost the company a fortune in the overall projects expenses. The non-financial has only a small guaranteed loss in the money paid to the insurance company to insure it. Types of insurable risk include such areas as contractual failure or lawsuits.

Risk quantification

Risk Quantification involves evaluating risks and risk interactions to assess the range of possible outcomes. This is necessary in order to estimate the impact on a project or a business. The impact of a risk is dependent on the likelihood of occurrence and the importance of the risk. This is shown mathematically below:

Impact of a risk $= f$ (likelihood of risk, severity of risk).

Table 5.5. Severity of risk summary table.

Severity Index	Financial (e.g. Bond portfolio trading)	Non-Financial (e.g. Environmental impact of toxic chemicals)
10	Loss of entire capital	Death
8	Loss of nearly all capital trading terminated	Permanent severe incapacity
6	Loss of 65% of capital trading restricted	Absent from work for more than 3 weeks with subsequent recurring incapacity
4	Some loss of capital 30% but recovery possible through re-trading	Absent from work for more than 3 days but less than 3 weeks with subsequent complete recovery
2	Small loss of capital 5% complete recovery expected	Minor injury with no lost time and complete recovery

Table 5.6. Probability of risk summary table.

Probability (out of 1000)	Descriptive Phrases
1000	Inevitable
950	Almost certain
900	Very likely
750	Probable
600	More than even chance
500	Even chance
400	Less than even chance
100	Improbable
50	Very improbable
1	Almost impossible

The principle concern of risk quantification is deciding whether or not a certain risk warrants a response or not. However, a number of factors can lead to complications in this decision.

The first step in quantifying risks is to assign a value to the elements describing risk. For example, when evaluating the severity of a risk, several possibilities can be classed according to a severity index. The same can be done with the likelihood of something happening.

The second step of risk quantifying is to assign the probability of the risk occurring. This can be done by statistically analysing data collected over time. If the data does not exist, however, questioning people working closer to the risk may give some idea of its likelihood.

Example of mathematical approach

After risk identification and quantification, the relevant data that have been accumulated should contain the likelihood and the impact of the risks as management sees them. They can then be sorted according to the level of how critical they are with respect to the project. Matrices can then be created from the data that have been gathered.

Figure 5.4 represents the likelihood probability as

- VL: Rare
- L: Possible
- M: Likely
- H: Almost certain

and the severity as

- VL: low financial losses; service delivery unaffected, no legal implications; unlikely to affect the environment, unlikely to damage reputation.
- L: medium financial losses; reprioritising of delivery required; minor legal implications; minor environmental impact, short term reputation damage
- M: major financial losses; deadlines renegotiated with customers; potentially serious legal implications; significant environmental impact, long term reputation damage

Likelyhood				
H	M	M	H	H
M	L	M	M	H
L	L	L	M	M
VL	L	L	L	M
	VL	L	M	H

Severity

Figure 5.4. Boston matrix for risk.

- H: huge financial losses; key deadlines missed with customers; very serious legal implications; major environmental impact, loss of public confidence

The process of deciding which risk is most critical is simple, as it will be a simple combination of the likelihood and the severity:

Risk mitigation

This is at the heart of Risk Management and involves responding to risks in an appropriate way with regard to the overall objectives of the project. This will mean revising the project plan with regard to such areas as schedule, quality, budget and purpose and then making a judgement call depending on how adversely the risk could affect the project, if it was to occur. There are a number of circumstances, which can influence a potential decision or make it difficult to respond at all.

The approaches for risk reduction or control fall into four broad categories of actions (see Figure 5.5):

- live with
- contain and control
- contingency plan or insurance
- prevention

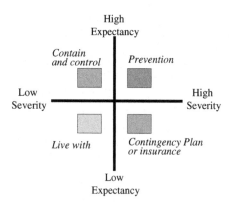

Figure 5.5. Severity versus expectancy plot.

Table 5.7. Frequency index scale.

Frequency Index	Financial (e.g. Bond portfolio trading)	Non-Financial (e.g. Environmental impact of toxic chemicals)
10	Trading loss at any time	Hazard permanently present
8	Trading loss every minute	Hazard arises every minute
6	Trading loss arises every hour	Hazard arises every hour
4	Trading loss by a new trader at next shift	Hazard arises at every shift
2	Portfolio re-balanced trading loss every month	Hazard arises every month
1	Bond default trading loss every year	Hazard arises every year

These actions arise from the previous risk matrix, and consider a different type of risk-management action depending on the position on the severity/probability plot.

However, building on the conclusions by Mitra (Mitra, 2003), we should take into account the effect of the frequency that adverse event might occur. Once again a scoring can be introduced to secure this concept on a more solid mathematical ground. The effect of frequency is that one to move across the action diagram in Figure 5.5 diagonally.

We shall explain this concept by using a simple example from the food business: our business sells chocolate cakes. As part of the key recipe, one must include ingredients such as:

– flower	250 grams
– eggs	4 unit
– milk	if necessary
– fats	125 grams
– sugar	300 grams
– chocolate powder	50 grams
– vanilla extract	1 tea spoon
– yeast	1 tea spoon

Some of these are critical ingredients, such as chocolate powder (without chocolate, we cannot make a chocolate cake!), other are key ingredients such as flour, sugar and yeast (high volume, high spend), some can be

93

substituted — with no impact on the final product such as fats (as we could use margarine as well as butter) and finally some are included simply as 'fillers' such as milk or vanilla flavouring.

We shall consider five examples of how the action will change according to an increase frequency of the adverse event.

Low severity, low expectancy

The supplier, who produces a substitute-type material, say fats, operates in a purely open and competitive market. There are plenty of alternative suppliers we could consider, and plenty of alternative types of fats that we could use in our recipe. In assessing the risk that an adverse event will stop business production and, therefore, our supply of fats, we have assessed a L,L impact on the matrix, which leads to a 'live-with' action.

However, if the frequency of going out of business of a supplier increases in that specific market, our choice of potential suppliers is drastically reduced, and we move towards a contingency plan, in the High Severity, Low Expectancy of the diagram.

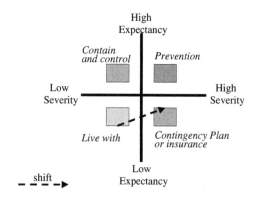

Figure 5.6. Frequency impact in Example (1).

High severity, low expectancy

The supplier, who produces a key material, say yeast, operates in an open and competitive market. There are plenty of alternative suppliers we could

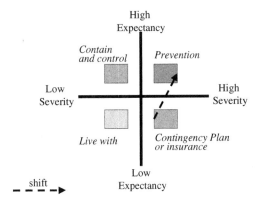

Figure 5.7. Frequency impact in Example (2).

consider, but we cannot substitute yeast with anything else! In assessing the risk that an adverse event will stop the production of our supplier, we have taken preventive actions and signed a back-up contract with an alternative supplier. This is a typical example of contingency plan in place.

However, if the frequency of going out of business of suppliers in this field increases, our contingency plan is not enough, and we need to take more drastic actions, such as form a partnership with both suppliers, and prevent then from falling into financial difficulties.

We move towards the top right corner of the diagram, with an action of prevention.

Low severity, high expectancy

The supplier, who produces a filler-type material, say vanilla extract, operates in a niche market. There are only few suppliers of vanilla extract, but this is such a minor addition to our recipe that we could still continue our chocolate cake business even without that specific aroma in the end product.

In assessing the risk that an adverse event will stop the production of our supplier, we have decided to contain and control, and only monitor the situation.

However, if the frequency of going out of business of these niche suppliers in this field increases, our monitoring is not enough, and we may decide

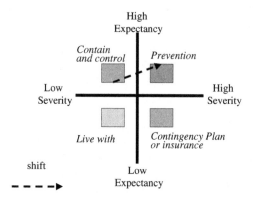

Figure 5.8. Frequency impact in Example (3).

to take preventive actions such as developing an alternative formulation using vanilla flavour.

We move towards the top right corner of the diagram, with an action of prevention.

Low severity, low expectancy

We should revisit the first example, because things might take a different course of action. The suppliers of different types of fats abound in this open and competitive market. We had taken a decision to live-with the risk of some of them going out of business.

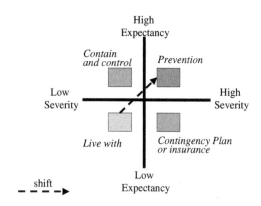

Figure 5.9. Frequency impact in Example (4).

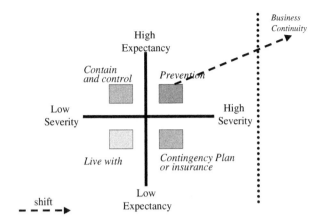

Figure 5.10. Frequency impact in Example (5).

However, external pressures in the market could arise, for example the Mediterranean type diet could become very popular. Consumers are less willing to buy cakes baked with saturated or polyunsaturated fat such as butter or margarine and prefer mono-unsaturated fat as olive oil. Therefore, we are pushed to use extra virgin oil exclusively. Fat is not a substitute material anymore and if the frequency of going out of business of extra virgin oil suppliers in this field would increase, our 'live-with' strategy can be fatal, and we should decide to take preventive actions, once again, forming a partnership with one or two potential suppliers and prevent then from falling into financial difficulties.

We move towards the top right corner of the diagram, with an action of prevention.

High severity, high expectancy

In the last example, we already start from the top right corner or the diagram, where we are already in prevention mode.

Here, we have strong links with a chocolate powder producer. If they go out of business, even after all the prevention measures we have taken, we cannot produce chocolate cakes anymore.

In case frequency of these adverse events is too high, then we should consider taking drastic actions, to ensure business continuity, and turn our production towards a different type of product, say lemon cakes!

Frequency induced corrective actions

In mathematical terms we could summarise the series of previous examples in a diagonal movement across the risk-action diagram, so that the new action is a function of the (low frequency) planned action and the increased frequency effect:

New action = old action × f (frequency).

To a first approximation, the function of frequency is linear, as it would move across the diagram as a straight line from bottom-left to top-right. In this sense, the severity would increase linearly, as would the expectancy.

$$S \Rightarrow S + \Delta S$$

$$E \Rightarrow E + \Delta E$$

Therefore, the new position (E′, S′) with respect to the old (E, S) in the plane will be given by

$$E' - E = dE/dS \times (S' - S),$$

where the slope dE/dS is a positive constant of order one.

Risk index

As we have discussed, risk analysis is at the heart of effective decision-making process. It comprises three basic steps. First, the identification of the

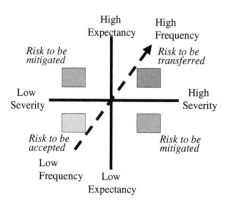

Figure 5.11. Risk and decision making.

critical areas, their impact on the business, and recovery time and objectives. Second, the evaluation of the vulnerability of critical threats that could exploit them. Finally, the risk assessment combines this information and assesses possible countermeasures to be used to minimise risk.

Based on this assessment, it is possible to formulate an indicator that reflects the level of risk of the project:

- risk to be accepted (can be managed by the decision maker)
- risk to be mitigated (safeguards need to be put in place for the risk to be managed)
- risk to be transferred (to a higher level of decision making level)

Reflection on Learnings

"What three (or four) lessons have we learned?"

1. In making a sound decision, one needs to capture all the non-financial (strategic) sources of value growth within a prospective project. We identified the value of a project to be based on two major elements: Operational Value and Business Value. This is the growth matrix. The relative importance and content of each of these matrices depends on unique set of circumstances facing each project and the company's involved.

2. In supporting decision making under uncertain conditions, the business manager needs to take into account the minimum risk. All risks must be identified and assessed to ensure that they do not adversely affect the business decisions. Risks can be categorised into two categories such as financial and non-financial.

3. The financial risks contains any type of opportunity for a profit or a loss, such as investing in a new product line, which may, at the end of the day, either sell well and make a profit for the company or not sell at all and have cost the company a fortune in the overall projects expenses. The non-financial risk is much more difficult to identity and to control. This is at the heart of Risk Management and involves responding to risks in an appropriate way within the overall objectives of the project. This means revising the project plan with regard to such areas as schedule, quality, budget and purpose and then making a judgement call depending on how adversely the risk could affect the project, if it was to occur.

"How do I put them into practical application?"

A. We have prepared a sample project evaluation questionnaire based on the Operational and the Business Growth Matrices. Through these applied questionnaires, one can proceed and score the different elements, which captures the selected strategic thrusts.

B. After risk identification and quantification, the relevant data should contain the likelihood and the impact of the risks as management sees them.

They can then be sorted according to the level of how critical they are with respect to the project into a two dimensional diagram (likelihood vs. severity).

C. The approaches for risk reduction or control fall into four broad categories of actions:

- live with
- contain and control
- contingency plan or insurance
- prevention

The effect of frequency is that one to move across the action diagram diagonally, therefore the resulting action should change.

6

THE FRAMEWORK

Timely and comprehensive project evaluation and selection is a critical competence. Project evaluation is dominated by dated financial and residual income methodologies (*e.g.* payback, NPV, SVA, EVA). Business performance measurement research has been at best qualitative and focused on operational efficiency. These techniques are usually applied on an *ex post* basis (*e.g.* operations auditing) or in a detached corporate setting (*e.g.* strategic planning). We propose a framework for sound project evaluation: Project Applied Differential Operational Value Added (PADOVA).

The Vision

Our goals are:

- To ensure consideration of key strategic issues at the outset of each project.
- To propose several ways to enhance and correct the biases of the existing residual income methodologies.
- To provide a series of indicators (including risk assessment) to support the manager decision.

Our vision is to address all the common shortcomings and integrate many of the Business Performance Measures advances directly into project evaluation ensuring that the consideration of key strategic issues is done at the outset of each project.

Residual Income Indicator

The first component of the tool is a Residual Income indicator measure, which is based on hard financial data: cash flow from operations.

The standard starting point for Residual Income financial indicators (such as Shareholder Value Added) are the value drivers: cash in, cash out, weighted average cost of capital, etc. The creation of economic value tends to be a function of these value drivers. In this traditional framework, value added is equal to the terminal value plus the sum of discounted cash flow during the forecast period, minus the current value of the business. We propose several improvements.

The first one is on the plan, or forecast, value. The NPV is based on a prediction of cash flow. Uncertainty affects the predictability of the forecast. So cash flow predictions at short times are to be trusted more than predictions at longer times. We propose the use of an enhanced discount factor, based of similarities with the physics of random motion. As a consequence, fast return projects are promoted with respect to late return projects.

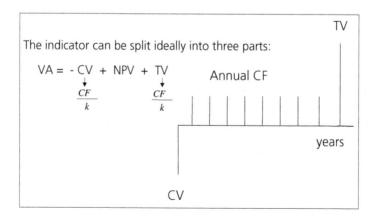

Figure 6.1. Traditional value added calculations.

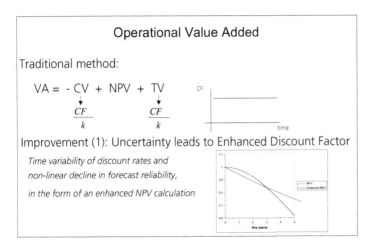

Figure 6.2. Improvement on the discounting procedure.

The second improvement is again on plan value evaluation. In traditional forecasting plans, there is no room for management flexibility. We introduced a real options approach to put some quantitative value on the operational flexibility, for example the option to grow or shrink the investment. Including flexibility, as expected, enhances the numerical value of the value added.

The third improvement is on the current and terminal value. The old approach is simple perpetuity model. This is not a good model in a highly competitive scenario. In the 1960s a base formulation for powder detergent lasted for 30 years. Now we are lucky if it lasts more than 6 months, or up to 1 year. So we propose to use a cut-off time, at which the business is not expected to produce any substantial operating cash flow.

We are interested in project evaluation. When you are comparing two projects, you only look at the difference in cash flow from operations. We define the Differential Operational Value Added as $CV = 0$ (since this is a differential measure).

The enhanced NPV is enriched with the real options calculation:

• Time variability of discount rates and non-linear decline in forecast reliability, in the form of an enhanced NPV calculation.

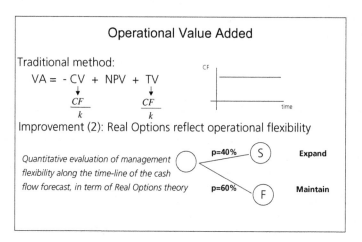

Figure 6.3. Introduction of real options to quantify flexibility.

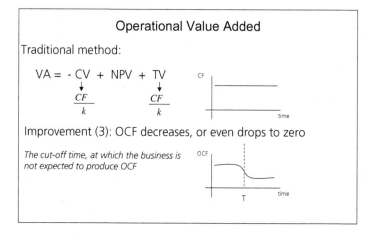

Figure 6.4. Going beyond the perpetuity model.

- Quantitative evaluation of management flexibility along the time-line of the cash flow forecast, in term of Real Options theory.

Plus the improved approximation of the terminal value, where we have included the concept of the cut-off time into the 'profitability parabola'. This is the time at which the business is not expected to produce OCF.

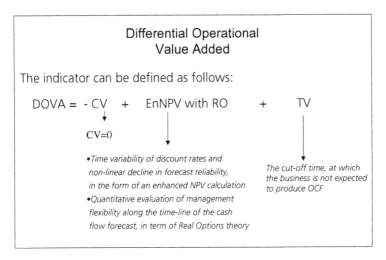

Figure 6.5. Summary of differential value added calculation.

Capital Scale Index

The second component of PADOVA is the capital scale index. In the modern business arena, we are confronted with a wealth of forms of collaborations, such as outsourcing, supply and logistics partnerships. One needs to weigh the capital involved in the investment. Traditional profitability index, which is defined at return on Investment, is not enough. We have introduced a stronger-than-linear dependence on the capital invested.

Growth Matrix

Project evaluation metrics often ignore or fail to capture key considerations in corporate strategy, leading to a mismatch between strategic planning and actual operations.

To address these weaknesses, we follow Fine (Fine, 2002) in developing a strategy-oriented growth matrix, which captures non-financial sources of value growth within a prospective project.

This matrix is further divided into the operational and business growth matrices. The first concentrates on project elements impacting at the operational level: namely issues concerning effectiveness, efficiency and

A constant cost of capital k is a convenient assumption when estimating financial return (R), but in reality the cost of capital often depends on the amount of capital involved (I).

$$Pi = \frac{I}{R}$$

Improvement: stronger-than-linear dependence on capital invested

$$CSi = \frac{I \log(I)}{R}$$

	Example	
	Company A	Company B
Investment	1,000	100
Return	500	50
Profitability Index	2	2
Capital Scale Index	6	4

Figure 6.6. Capital scale index.

inter-project externalities. These categories are derived from standard operations management literature. The second concentrates on a project's broader impact at the business level. Then we utilise the Porterian (SCP) competitive forces framework (Porter, 1980) to look at the project's impact on industry structure and conduct. And lastly, we follow various recent authors in examining a project's impact on fundamental business characteristics. By this we mean the introduction of radical changes in the way companies operate and compete stemming from disruptive technologies, rapid information flow, etc.

In the end, we emphasise the holistic appraisal of any project, which would require an assiduous application of the entire matrix. The idea is to first translate, on a project-specific basis, these matrix categories into a set of critical success factors, which are then measured and weighed for their impact. The purpose is to fill gaps and oversights occurring within financial project evaluation. The complete matrix should be considered when evaluating projects.

Risk Analysis

The purpose is to fill the gaps within the financial evaluation and the strategic analysis. This is an assessment tool used to identify critical areas, evaluates

Operational and Business Growth Matrices

Strategic Project Evaluation	Operational Growth Matrix			Business Growth Matrix			
	Operational Effectiveness	Operational Efficiency	Operational Externalities	Resource Accumulation	Capability Development	Industry Structure/Conduct	Business Characteristics
Product Development (Processes)	Does the product development pipeline offer the right products at the right time?	Are the product development processes optimised for lead-time, costs, etc.?	Makes development of other products more effective or efficient?	Acquire/develop useful product development resources?	Build and refine new or existing product development capabilities?	Can improved product development processes alter industry structure or level of competition?	Fundamentally alter product characteristics (usage, content, technology, etc.)?
Product Delivery	Provide competitive cost, dependability, flexibility, quality, and speed? Achieve continuous product/process improvement?	Actively eliminate waste? Pursue lean? Achieve continuous cost reduction?	Makes delivery of other products more effective or efficient?	Acquire/develop useful product delivery resources?	Build and refine new or existing product delivery capabilities?	Can improved product delivery processes alter industry structure or level of competition?	Fundamentally alter product delivery processes (channels, production techniques, logistics, etc.)?
Customer Involvement (Linkages)	Does the project maximise customer interaction and responsiveness?	Are mechanisms for customer interaction optimally coordinated?	Facilitates customer involvement on other projects?	Acquire/develop resources for effective customer involvement (i.e. power, trust, IT, data, habits, image)	Develop or improve channels/mechanisms for customer interaction?	Does customer involvement promote a more favourable industry structure or reduce competition?	Fundamentally alter nature of customers' interaction with the product and the firm?
Supply Chain Management	Does the project promote supply chain management best practices? Will suppliers be able to contribute significant additional value?	Are supplier best practices, monitoring, and involvement optimally coordinated?	Facilitates supply chain management on other projects?	Acquire/develop resources for effective supply chain mgmt (i.e. personnel, IPTs, IT, trust, power)	Develop or improve channels/mechanisms /routines for supply chain management?	Do supply chain practices promote a more favourable industry structure or reduce competition?	Fundamentally alter nature of supplier roles on the project and with the firm?

Figure 6.7. The growth matrices.

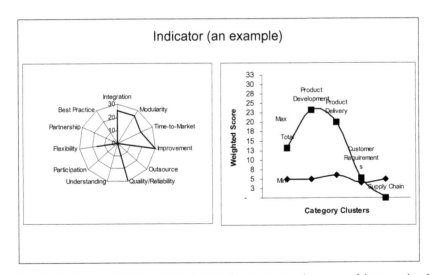

Figure 6.8. An example of growth indicator, where we report the scores of the operational growth indicator.

109

the impact of their loss on the business as well as the vulnerability of critical threats that could exploit them and assesses possible countermeasures to be used to minimise risk.

Based on this assessment, it is possible to formulate an indicator that reflects the level of risk of the project:

- risks to be accepted,
- risk to be mitigated and
- risk to be transferred.

Summary

Therefore, we have introduced a new framework and tool for evaluating project, this includes:

- Financial indicators improved by

    - Enhanced NPV,
    - Growth and shrink real options and
    - Profitability Parabola.

- Capital Scale Index with an higher sensitivity on Capital Investment involved and

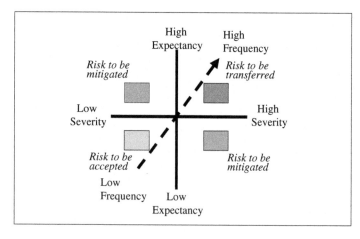

Figure 6.9. Risk analysis.

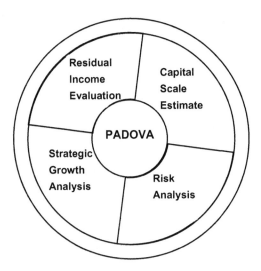

Figure 6.10. Schematic representation of PADOVA elements.

- Strategic Grow Matrices and Risk Analysis with semi-quantitative strategy based assessment tools

PADOVA proposes a more holistic picture of project value than possible when using other existing methods.

Reflection on Learnings

"What three (or four) lessons have we learned?"

1. Timely and comprehensive project evaluation and selection is a critical competence. Project evaluation is dominated by dated financial and residual income methodologies (*e.g.* payback, NPV, SVA, EVA).
2. Our goals are:
   - To ensure consideration of key strategic issues at the outset of each project.
   - To propose several ways to enhance and correct the biases of the existing residual income methodologies.
   - To include risk assessment and indicators to ensure that they do not adversely affect the manager decision.
3. Our vision is to address these common shortcomings and integrate many of Business Performance Measures advances directly into project evaluation ensuring that consideration of key strategic issues at the outset of each project.

"How do I put them into practical application?"

A. We have introduced a new framework and tool for evaluating projects, this includes a number of elements specified above.
B. PADOVA proposes a holistic approach to project evaluation. However, one can decide to use any PADOVA's element in isolation. In doing so, complexity and effort in input need to be commensurated with the gravity of the decision (impact).

7

IMPLEMENTING A CASE ILLUSTRATION

Residual Income Indicator

Using the case described in Figure 7.1, we illustrate the financial portion of the PADOVA framework, and compare it to popular indicators, such as Shareholder Value Added (SVA), Economic Value Added (EVA), NPV, DCF Yield, PI. Financial data of a hypothetical project scenario are shown (Table 7.1). This example also contains a management option at year 3. In Table 7.2, we look into the calculation for each financial indicator. We have compared the traditional EVA, SVA and Total Business Return (TBR) to the Enhanced Operational Value Added (EnOVA). The traditional measurements predict an increase in the value created as the forecast time window increases (some more linearly than others). On the contrary EnOVA shows that the value created is less as the time span increases. The longer the forecast-time, the larger the uncertainty on the predicted OCF. This is reflected on a lower value created in EnOVA.

In year 3, management has to take a decision whether to either expand or reduce the project. The decision will increase or decrease, respectively, the Cash Flow by 50%. Also the additional investment to go either way is equal to 50% of the total capital employed initially. Finally, the probability

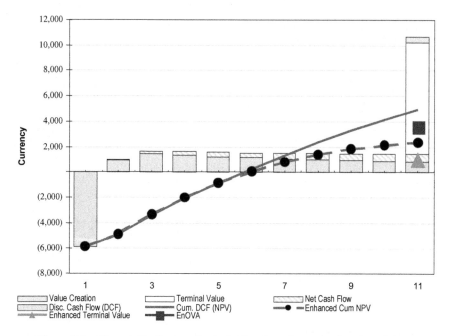

Figure 7.1. Financial indicators chart, plotting the value as the function of time.

that management will decide to expand the business is 60%, whereas the probability to reduce the activity is 40%.

The first part of Table 7.2 shows how the elements of the business case are evaluated according to traditional indicators and new ones. Since this is a differential analysis, the current value has been arbitrarily set to zero in all cases. Differences enter the computation at the plan value and terminal value prediction. The Plan Value calculation in EnOVA increases less rapidly than in the other methods, where a linear increase is clearly noticeable. This is in line with the enhanced discount procedure outlined before, which promotes OCF at short times, and penalises OCF at long times. In a similar way, one can concentrate on the Terminal Value analysis. The EVA approach to the estimate of the Terminal Value is substantially different and it increases with time, because of its cumulative character. On the contrary both SVA and TBR rely on a perpetuity model, which reflects

Table 7.1. Hypothetical project scenario (years 0 to 10).

	Differential Impact												
	year 0	year 1	year 2	year 3	year 4	year 5	year 6	year 7	year 8	year 9	year 10	year 11	Total
Sales (k€)	0	0	0	0	0	0	0	0	0	0	0	0	0
Operating Expenses	0	2,918	-124	-1,387	-1,554	-1,681	-1,775	-1,847	-1,900	-1,940	-1,970	-1,993	-13,253
Net Operating Profit	0	-2,918	124	1,387	1,554	1,681	1,775	1,847	1,900	1,940	1,970	1,993	13,253
Interest expense	0	0	0	0	0	0	0	0	0	0	0	0	0
Net profit before taxes	0	-2,918	124	1,387	1,554	1,681	1,775	1,847	1,900	1,940	1,970	1,993	13,253
Taxes @ 31%	0	-905	38	430	482	521	550	573	589	601	611	618	4,108
Net Profit after taxes	0	-2,013	86	957	1,072	1,160	1,225	1,274	1,311	1,339	1,359	1,375	9,145
Debt	0	0											0
Equity	0	4,973											4,973
Capital	0	4,973	0	0	0	0	0	0	0	0	0	0	4,973
NPAT	0	-2,013	86	957	1,072	1,160	1,225	1,274	1,311	1,339	1,359	1,375	9,145
Equity	0	4,973	0	0	0	0	0	0	0	0	0	0	4,973
ROE	n/a	-40.5%	n/a	n/a	n/a	n/a	n/a	n/a	n/a	n/a	n/a	n/a	183.9%
NPAT		-2,013	86	957	1,072	1,160	1,225	1,274	1,311	1,339	1,359	1,375	9,145
Interest expense	0	0	0	0	0	0	0	0	0	0	0	0	0
(Tax saved on interest)	0	0	0	0	0	0	0	0	0	0	0	0	0
NOPAT	0	-2,013	86	957	1,072	1,160	1,225	1,274	1,311	1,339	1,359	1,375	9,145
Capital	0	4,973	0	0	0	0	0	0	0	0	0	0	4,973
r (NOPAT/CAPITAL)	n/a	-40.5%	n/a	n/a	n/a	n/a	n/a	n/a	n/a	n/a	n/a	n/a	183.9%
Depreciation		*1,213*	*917*	*694*	*527*	*400*	*306*	*234*	*181*	*141*	*111*	*88*	*-4,812*
Cash Flow		*-5,846*	*1,003*	*1,651*	*1,599*	*1,560*	*1,531*	*1,508*	*1,492*	*1,480*	*1,470*	*1,463*	*8,911*

115

Table 7.2. Financial indicators required by different evaluation approaches.

Net operating profit (2009)	1,994
NOP after Tax & Finacing charge (2009)	1,376
Discounted payback	4.7 yrs
DCF yield (IRR)	21.0%
Profitability index	1.8
Capital scale index	*0.7*
NPV @ 6.0%	4,963
Enhanced NPV @ 6.0%	*2,362*
Total Business Return (TBR)	26.6%
Value Created (TBR)	10,651
Operation Value Added (EnOVA)	*3,577*
Economic Value Added (EVA)	16,056
Sahreholder Value Added (SVA)	17,843

in a gentle reduction of TV in time (due to the discounting effect). A more aggressive reduction in the TV, over and above the enhanced discounting procedure, is calculated in the EnOVA, and rests on the concept of the 'profitability parabola'.

Growth Matrix

The strategic growth matrices are implemented through a set of questionnaires, which translate the sources of value into operational criteria (see Figures 7.2–7.3). Significant scores are given in a scale from 0 to 5 for each question and then weighted according to the relative importance assigned to the specific areas. The relative weights, 1–7, have to be decided at the strategic level, with the attempt to give a mathematical support to the prioritisation of the strategy into action. This "filter mask" should be updated when the priorities have changed, and the organisation is pushing towards a different growth paradigm. We compare average score of each category with predefined threshold value and construct growth index accordingly, *e.g.* Very High, High, Medium and Low.

Operational growth				
	Score [0–5]	Mask [1–7]	Impact	Average
Product development				23
Integration	5	5	25	
Modularity	5	5	25	
Time-to-market	4	5	20	
Product delivery				20
Improvement	5	6	30	
Outsource	0	6	0	
Quality/reliability	5	6	30	
Customer requirements				5
Understanding	0	4	0	
Participation	0	4	0	
Flexibility	4	4	16	
Supply chain				0
Partnership	0	5	0	
Best practice	0	5	0	
Growth indicator (factor)				High

 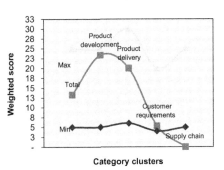

Figure 7.2. Example of operational growth.

Risk Analysis

The risk analysis is implemented through a questionnaire, which translates the sources of risk into operational criteria. Significant scores are given for severity, which measures the impact that the project can have on the business in a scale from 2 to 10, where 2 was the lowest impact. Expectancy, which is the probability that a certain factor will inhibit the project success, is scored in a scale from 1 to 1000, where 1 represents the lowest probability. Average score of each category constructs the first risk analysis index accordingly to risk reduction or control, *e.g.* live with, contain

Business growth				
	Score [0–5]	Mask [1–7]	Impact	Average
Product development				20
Leading brands	4	5	20	
Modular design	4	5	20	
Product capability	4	5	20	
Intelectual property	4	5	20	
Product delivery				24
Process capability	4	6	24	
Process innovation	4	6	24	
Workforce improvement	4	6	24	
Customer requirements				12
Multi-local multinational	3	4	12	
Market leadership	3	4	12	
Brand reputation	3	4	12	
Supply chain				20
Future operations	4	5	20	
Suppliers relationship	4	5	20	
Level of competition	4	5	20	
Growth indicator (factor)				**High**

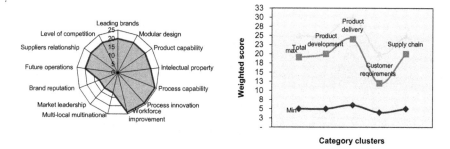

Figure 7.3. Example of business growth.

and control, contingency plan or insurance, and prevention. These actions depend on the position on the severity/probability plot and consider the different type of risk-management action.

The effect of the frequency that an adverse event might occur is taken into account. Once again the scoring is used with a scale from 1 to 10, where 1 is the lowest frequency.

The average score of each category make up the final risk analysis indicator informing the decision-making process, *e.g.* risk to be accepted or to be mitigated or to be transferred.

Table 7.3. Risk analysis questionnaire.

Risk Analysis

Project Name:	Case Illustration
Date:	

	Type	Section	Items	Definition	Severity Index	Expectancy scale	Frequency scale
1	Enablers	Innovation/New Technology	Vulnerability	Exposure to serious business disruption, arising from risks within the supply chain as well as risks external to the supply chain	2	100	10
2	Enablers	Technical Expertise	Technical and Professional skills and feasibility	Available internal and external resources required skills	2	100	10
3	Enablers	Customer Knowledge	Customer Intimacy	Consumer driven development Extent of benefit received through customer contact Maintenance costs Customer loyalty	2	100	10
4	Enablers	Reputation/Brand Development	Brands, trademarks, goodwill	Presence of competing brands Extent of perceived differences Price premium commanded Price commanded when sold	2	1000	10
5	Enablers	Supply Chain Development/ Relations	Supplier Relations	Supplier willingness to cooperate Impact of supplier cooperation Cost reduction Compliance on cost-cutting initiatives Risk/investment sharing Reduced risk of hold-up	2	1	10
6	Enablers	External Relations	Government/ Customs Relations	Political risk Ability to resolve potential conflicts Risk of political or economic sanctions Possible govt subsidies or tariff protection	2	1	10
7	Enablers	External Relations	Regulatory Agencies Relations	Likelihood of product failure Extent of regulatory discretion Reduced product dvpt risk Faster product time-to-market	2	1	10
8	Enablers	External Relations	Community Relations	Importance of community support Firm's impact on community Reduced risk of adverse community action Lower hiring costs	2	1	10

	Type	Section	Items	Definition	Severity Index	Expectancy scale	Frequency scale
9	Enablers	Financial Resources	Investor Relations	Willingness to provide flexible financial terms Lower cost of capital Tolerance for long-term projects	2	1	10
10	Enablers	Organisation/ Mgmt Resources	Employee Relations	Willingness to support operations Flexibility of work/pay arrangements Reduced risk of labour disputes & work stoppage Lower cost of labour	2	1	10
11	Enablers	Scale/ Process Economies	Distribution of fixed costs	Leaner supply chains and just-in-time practices and globalisation of supply	2	1	10
12	Sustainers	Market Position	Growth renewal	Size of product market enhanced Extent of added growth Market share and revenues generated or sustained	2	1	10
13	Sustainers	Channel Domination	Availabilty (distribution)	Out of stock On shelf availability	2	1	10
14	Sustainers	Critical Technogy	Critical Technology	Development operational structure protection of IPR superior supply chain position	2	1	10
15	Sustainers	Supply Chain Positioning	Benefit ot the Customer	Reduce risk or operating costs	2	1	10
16	Sustainers	Product Differentiation	Product Quality/Reliability	Sustainability Extent of perceived differences	2	1	10
17	Sustainers	Superior Risk Management	Delayed decision time period Reduced commitment/sunk costs	Potential for failure Magnitude of investment Increased capital requirements Initial capital requirements Reduced capital investment	2	1	10
18	Sustainers	Lean/Operation Excellence	Employee Loyalty/Commitment	Degree of uncertainty in employment Potential for work disruption Reduced labour overheads Flexibility employment Superior quality and operations execution	2	1	10
19	Sustainers	Operational Flexibility	Cross-project risk reduction	Uncertainty and variability in operations Supplier power Reduced cost of capital Reduced operating and insurance costs	2	1	10
					38	1315	190

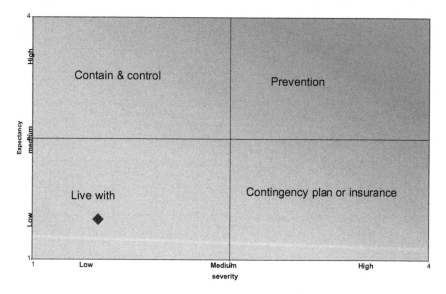

Figure 7.4. Risk analysis.

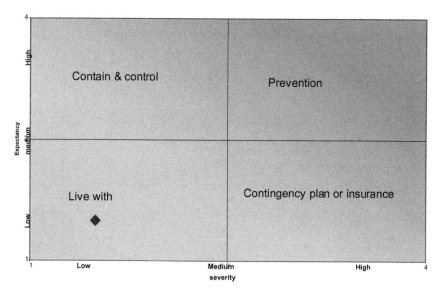

Figure 7.5. Risk analysis with frequency.

Reflection on Learnings

"What three (or four) lessons have we learned?"

1. PADOVA is a framework which can be applied to a realistic case study to give a set of indicators that will be used jointly to assess the project.
2. We illustrate the financial portion of the PADOVA framework, and compare it to popular indicators, such as SVA, EVA. The financial data are taken from of a 10 year hypothetical project scenario, which contains a management option at year 3.
3. The strategic growth matrices were implemented through a set of questionnaires, which translate the sources of value into operational criteria. Significant scores are given for each question and then weighted according to the relative importance assigned to specific areas. These weights have to be decided at the strategic level, with the attempt to give a mathematical support to the prioritisation of the strategy into action. We compare average score of each category with predefined threshold value and construct growth index accordingly, *e.g.* Very High, High, Medium and Low.
4. The risk analysis is implemented through a questionnaire, which translates the sources of risk into operational criteria. Significant scores are given for severity. Expectancy is the probability that a certain factor will inhibit the project success. Average score of each category constructs the first risk analysis index accordingly to risk reduction or control. When frequency is taken into account, the average score of each category forms the final risk analysis indicator, which informs the decision-making process.

"How do I put them into practical application?"

Look back at this case illustration, and just give it a try with you own data!

CONCLUSIONS

A WAY FORWARD

The conditions for making decisions can be divided into two types, certainty and uncertainty. Decisions made under certainty or uncertainty are based both on our feelings and our experiences.

Certainty and Uncertainty

We experience certainty about a specific question when we have a feeling of complete belief or complete confidence in a single answer to the question. Decisions such as choosing a new carpet for the office or installing a new piece of equipment or promoting an employee to a supervisory position are made with a high level of certainty. While there is always some degree of uncertainty about the eventual outcome of such decisions there is enough clarity about the problem, the situation and the alternatives to consider the conditions to be certain.

The decision maker needs some skills and methods to make decisions under uncertainty. They need techniques that match the limited time and money budgets of the project. Most financial planning decisions are fraught with uncertainty. And making sound decisions has always been very difficult.

At the present moment, making these decisions has become even more difficult. There is less time to make a decision in a business world that has become ever more dynamic. The playing field has become so broad and enriched by many new entrants. The barriers for entering the market have been lowered, and new players are easily coming into the picture. There are plenty of companies that can offer cheap alternatives, because most of the products can be quickly copied or reengineered at low cost.

On top of this, we should mention that there are several pulls in orthogonal directions to advice the decision maker on different dimensions to be optimised or maximised, in order to support the decision making process. A school of thought is pressing for maximising added value, while another will strive for economic value; one might embrace the philosophy of growth, and another might concentrate on minimising risk.

Influencing Factors

Decision making has become more difficult, and decision-making process is even more vulnerable.

Personal psychology of the decision maker

This is the attitude of the decision maker and their drive, attitude towards risk and personal preference towards intuition versus analytical analysis.

For example, it is the decision maker's tolerance to risk that might drive the decision, and it must be examined. Three commonly used classifications for risk appear in the diagram below. They include the

— risk averter or avoider,
— neutral risk taker and
— risk seeker or lover.

The following diagram illustrates decision-makers curves where the y-axis represents the "utility" or the amount of satisfaction received from a payoff (the business manager's tolerance for risk) and the x-axis is the amount of money at stake.

The shape of a given decision-makers curve is derived from comparing responses to alternative decisions. A risk averter, as shown by the diagram, is someone who avoids risk more and more as the money at stake increases. A neutral risk taker makes a balanced decision on the risk calculated from

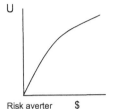 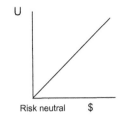 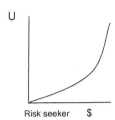

Figure 8.1. Decision-makers curves (Kerzner, 1998).

its probabilities and the possible gains or losses from such a decision. A risk seeker is more likely to take the decision if there is a larger sum at stake.

Likewise, a decision maker can be driven to follow their instincts or to support the decision on a solid block of data.

Data-driven decision making can be achieved at different levels. When we drill down into the detailed data using more sophisticated analyses, we often uncover new and important information that can be persuasive enough to move us to action. When that data address a need or concern, we act.

Persuasive data, data that move us to take action, come in two forms: the big picture data and the details that show us what, if anything, should be changed. When we have these data — the details that provide a complete picture — we are likely to decide to do something productive, something that benefits the business.

Even with drill-down analysis, however, we rarely come to a clear and concise decision point. Often, we learn more about the problem and potential solution, thereby better "informing our intuition" about what needs to be improved. Data-driven decision-making analysis adds to that knowledge base and provides a clearer pathway to action.

At the first lever, data-supported analysis relies on the aggregate reporting of roll-up averages, such as "score cards". Displaying how one business performed as compared with others paints a big picture of market effectiveness and progress, but it does not provide the data for the "drill-down" detailed analyses we need to determine if change is necessary.

At a more detailed level, the analysis-minded decision maker uses more in-depth analyses based on detailed, specific and relevant business data and includes reporting based on these analyses. The initial conclusions drawn from the first level or reports are often misleading and downright wrong when subsequently analysed more deeply. However, for these reports to be truly useful, all of this number crunching needs to be followed up with observation and interviews to help us better understand trends and drive potential actions. The reports provide a useful compass direction for decisions, but often do not lead to specific and discernible actions.

That may sound curious, if not frustrating, as one would think that after all this work a decision or direction should become obvious. Occasionally that does happen, but not often. It is a lot like buying that car: at the end of all the analyses we are still left with a tough and personal decision.

With the results of the detailed analyses, decision makers can begin to discuss not just the big picture, but the minute details of what is really going on in the business. It is those discussions about the relevance of the data that are the persuasion factor. Meaningful actions and changes are the results.

Scope of the decision

A decision under uncertainty is when there are many unknowns and no possibility of knowing what could occur in the future to alter the outcome of a decision. We feel uncertainty about a situation when we cannot predict with complete confidence what the outcomes of our actions will be. We experience uncertainty about a specific question when we cannot give a single answer with complete confidence. Launching a new product, a major change in marketing strategy or opening your first branch could be influenced by such factors as the reaction of competitors, new competitors, technological changes, changes in customer demand, economic shifts, government legislation and a host of conditions beyond your control.

These are the type of decisions facing the decision makers of large corporations who must commit huge resources. The small business decision maker faces, relatively, the same type of conditions which could cause decisions that result in a disaster from which they may not be able to recover. Most often, the decision maker, (a) has little time for research, (b) does not need an exhaustive analysis, (c) can accept the risks and (d) can make reversible decisions. Large corporations may have millions of dollars for research, the risks may be highly punitive and commitments are not easily reversed.

Different tools and processes should be used to support decision making at different levels. Of course the decision maker should invest the proper amount of time and money on gathering data on the decision to be made, on a scale which is proportional to the impact of the decision.

External conditioning

Large and small businesses are influenced by latest fashions and trends in strategy, which are immediately followed and supported by an army of consultants, ready to provide specialised support to guide the strategic decisions according to the latest paradigms. These external conditionings are keen to colour the way in which decisions are made, ranging from purely financial methodologies (e.g. payback, NPV, SVA, EVA) to business performance measurement methodologies (more qualitative-oriented and more focussed on operational efficiency), to purely aseptic strategic settings in the high corporate spheres.

How can we Help the Decision-Making Process?

First, we should start from the realisation that the single magic indicator is more mythical than real. The magic number that gives solution single-handedly to all decision does not exist, and if it exists it is misleading. Our long experience in decision making within a major multinational corporation has allowed us to gather enough evidence that such single number is not useful either! What helps most a decision maker is the support of a suite of indicators, a mix of evaluations that encompasses several areas that concur to support the process of decision making, ranging from financial to strategic, to risk control, to capital impact.

Eventually it is the decision maker that elicits one option among all others, and takes the business decision. In this sense, the individual approach would be dominant, but supported by a range of support tools, which are there to help an informed decision.

A Framework for Taking Decisions

This work introduces the PADOVA decision tool, resulting from collaboration with Cambridge University — Institute for Manufacturing.

These metrics are a suite of tools, and the different indicators can be used independently. PADOVA may seem complicated, especially when tackling a simple situation with a low economic profile. However, we strongly suggest to use the entire suite of indicators because each one often sheds some light from a different angle.

While this work represents a good step forward in assisting decision-making process under uncertain business conditions, some areas remains open and prone to improvements. We recommend that more work should continue along a few lines:

— the quantitative representation of the financial impact and how to quantify risk
— the strategic business matrix, which is aimed at aligning with the growth business trends, needs to be synchronised with relevant strategic needs
— on the same theme, we need to understand the elements and sectors that generate profit, growth, increased sales, and how this can be linked in a feedback mechanism into the indicator
— more detail is needed to tailor the study to a specific sector or a specific brand area

There might be some friction towards the proposal of new tools for helping decision making. Protest against advances of new tools, be they machines or methods has been disputed by modern philosophers.

We trust our work is a contribution to progress in the area of the tools supporting decision making. However, we are also conscious that in the end tools are only there to help the decision maker. The wheels of the financial, risk and growth indicators are only there to help. They are not intended to take over the mind of the decision maker.

In the end, it is the decision maker who has indeed full control of the business decision and will take full responsibility and full credit for a job well done.

APPENDIX

In order to gain further confidence, the robustness of the proposed model was examined by challenging the residual income method, on the basis of the same case study reported in Chapter 7. We have chosen to test the model on a realistic case study, to verify that it makes sense for practical purposes and give us confidence that it can be used in real life applications. That is the value of the exercise in this appendix.

We have performed a number of simulations using different constraints. Typically, each analysis is focussed on one element of the model, everything else being equal. Not only are we interested in qualitative trends, but also on the relative magnitude of several elements: the quantitative comparison will inform the analyst on the real value in performing a quick-and-dirty evaluation or a detailed residual income analysis. It is reassuring to observe results that confirm the expected mathematical trends of the formulation and the insight matured after years of field experience in the area of applied project evaluation. The results and the term of comparison are reported in the charts detailed on the following pages.

Effect of Discounting Model

Given a fixed profile of the forecasted 10-year window operating cash flow, we calculated different residual income indicators at different times along the forecast window, in order to capture the trends of the value generated. The following chart portrays the OCF profile during the forecast period, and includes the classic discounted OCF, and the Enhanced discounted OCF. Note that the enhanced discounting procedure results in penalising the OCF at later times.

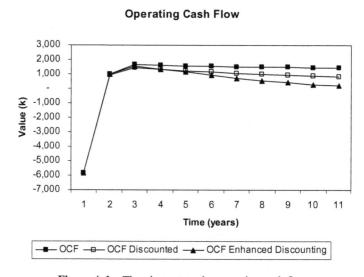

Figure A.1. Time impact on the operating cash flow.

Comparison of Different Residual Income Indicators on Value Creation

We compare the EVA and SVA, the TBR to the EnOVA. The classical residual income indicators predict an increase in the value created as the forecast time window increases. On the contrary EnOVA shows that the value created decreases at the time span increases. The longer the forecast-time, the larger the uncertainty on the predicted OCF. This is reflected on a lower value created in EnOVA.

Comparison of Different Residual Income Indicators on Plan Value

Since this is a differential analysis, the current value has been arbitrarily set to zero in all cases. Differences enter the computation at the plan value and terminal value prediction. In all cases the Plan Value increases with time.

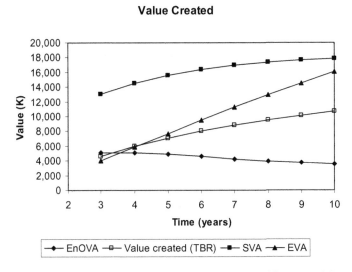

Figure A.2. Comparison of overall value created in different models.

The Plan Value calculation in EnOVA increases less rapidly than in the other methods, where a linear increase is clearly noticeable. This is in line with the enhanced discount procedure outline in previous chapters, which promotes OCF at short times, and penalises OCF in the long times.

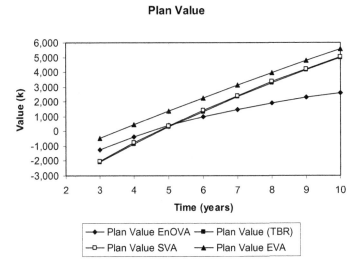

Figure A.3. Comparison of plan value created in different models.

Effect of Additional Flexibility (Real Options) onto the Plan Value

The calculation of the Plan Value on EnOVA includes a term originating from the Real Options theory, which includes management flexibility as an added value. The decision time is after 3 years, and a conservative approach has been taken in including the extra value generated by flexibility. It is not surprising that the extra value originating from flexibility is higher at times closed to year 3.

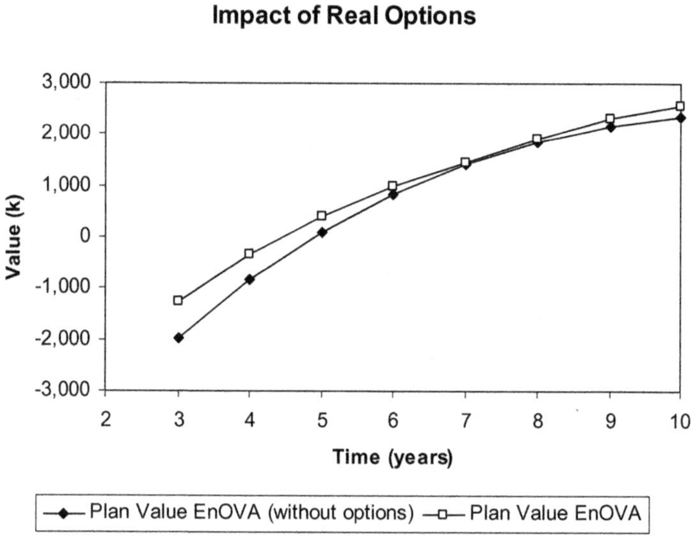

Impact of Real Options

Figure A.4. Impact of real options on two different models.

Comparison of Different Residual Income Indicators on Terminal Value

The EVA approach to the estimate of the Terminal Value is substantially different and it increases with time, because of its cumulative character. On the contrary both SVA and TBR rely on a perpetuity model, which reflects in a gentle reduction of TV in time (due to the discounting effect). A more aggressive reduction in the TV, over and above the enhanced discounting procedure, is calculated in the EnOVA, as it relies on the concept of the 'profitability parabola'.

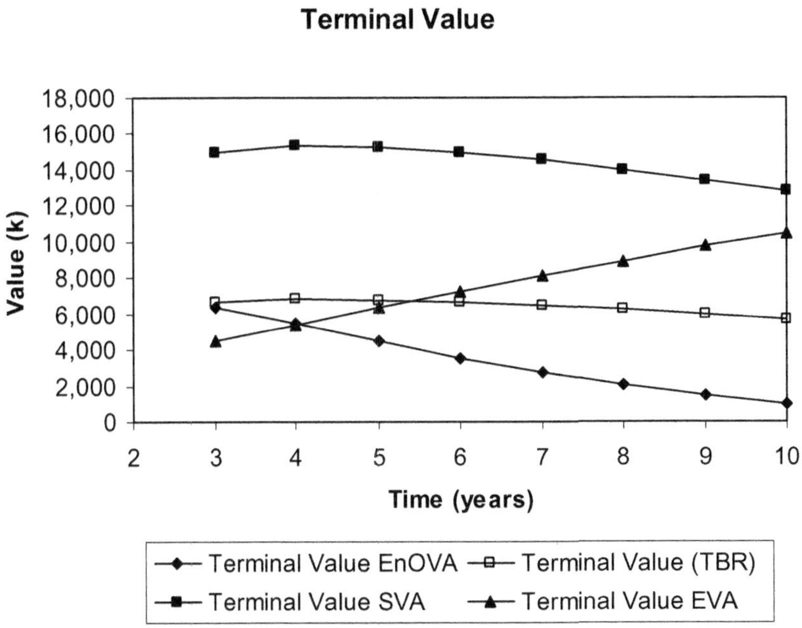

Terminal Value

Figure A.5. Impact of profitability parabola on the terminal value.

Effect of Initial Capital on Value Creation

Given a fixed 10-year total income and a fixed OCF distribution profile over the same time, we study the impact of a different initial capital investment in five different scenarios. The initial investment is varied in a relative manner with respect to the base case scenario, and its relative value is tracked by the multiplicative factor ranging from 0.1 to 10 (where Factor = 1 represents the base case). The Figure plots the NPV, the EPV, the Value Created in TBR and the Value Created in EnOVA as a function of the multiplicative factor. All these measures, with the exception of EnOVA, decrease linearly with the capital investment with the same slope. The Value Created in the EnOVA model still decreases with increasing capital commitment, but with a slower pace. We believe this is due to the fact that in EnOVA calculation more weight, relatively speaking, is assigned to the income rather than to the capital invested, because of the extra value

Capital Scale Impact

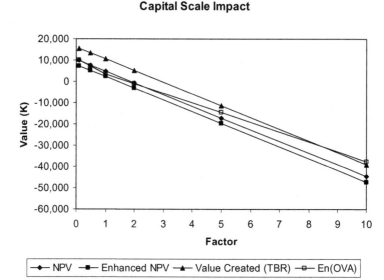

Figure A.6. Impact of capital investment on different models.

generated by the Real Options and because of the enhanced discounting method.

Comparison Between Profitability Index and Capital Scale Index

Given the same 10-year forecast, the same distribution, and the same capital, we now study the impact of the scale of the problem, where both the size of the income and the size of the capital invested are increased proportionally. Our motivation is to explore the concept of shared risk of capital and returns in case of a partnership. We have approached this problem by using the Profitability Index (PI), which is calculated as the present value of the cash receipts divided by the initial investment and the Capital Scale Index (CSI), which stresses the capital involvement. In the Figure A.7 we plot the PI and the CSI as a function of the Scale Factor. High scale factor means low size. It is cleat that PI remains constant throughout, while the CSI increases at the capital committed is less (high Scale Factors).

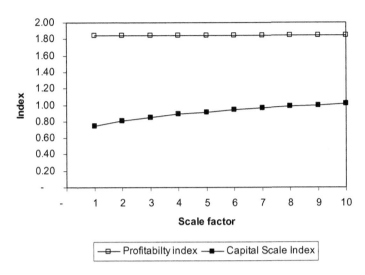

Figure A.7. Comparison of profitability index and capital scale index.

REFERENCES

Ansoff, H. I. (1968). *Corporate Strategy.* New York, Penguin.

Arnold, G. and M. Davies (eds) (2000). *Value-Based Management: Context and Application,* John Willy and Sons.

Besley, S. and E. F. Brigham (1999). *Principles of Finance,* Fort Worth, The Dryden Press.

Botzel, S. and A. Schwilling (1999). *Managing for Value,* Capstone.

Bovet, D. and J. Martha (2000). *Value Nets: Breaking the Supply Chain to Unlock Hidden Profits,* John Willy & Sons.

Brealey, R. A. and S. C. Myers (1991). *Principles of Corporate Finance,* (4th ed.), New York, McGraw-Hill, Inc.

Bromwich M. and A. Bhimani (1991). *Strategic Investment Appraisal Management Accounting,* March.

Donnellan, (2000). *PriceWater House Coopers.*

Doz, Y. L. and H. Gary (1998). *Alliance Advantage: The Art of Creating Value Through Partnering,* Boston: Harvard Business School Press.

Fine, C. H. (1998). *Clockspeed: Winning Industrial Control in the Age of Temporary Advantage,* London. Little, Brown and Company.

Fine, C. H., V. Roger *et al.* (2002). Rapid response capability in value chain design, *MIT Sloan Management Review,* Winter 69–75.

Hax, A. C. and L. W. Dean II (2001). *The Delta Project,* Houndmills, Palgrave.

Kaplan, R. S. and D. P. Norton (1996). Linking the balanced scorecard to strategy, *California Management Review* **39**, 53–80.

Kay, J. (1993). *Foundations of Corporate Success,* Oxford: Oxford University Press.

Lanning, M. J. (1998) *Delivering Profitable Value.* Oxford: Capstone.

Lynch, R. L. and K. F. Cross (1991). *Measure Up — The Essential Guide to Measuring Business Performance*. London: Mandarin.

Makelainen, E. (1998). Economic value added as a management tool, *Technical Report*, Helsinki School of Economics and Business Administration, 1–57.

Mitra, G. (2003). Decision Modelling and Information Systems — The Information Value Chain, Springer.

Neely, A. D., M. J. Gregory *et al.* (1995). Performance measurement system design: A literature review and research agenda, *International Journal of Operations and Production Management* **15**, 80–116.

Normann, R. and R. Rafael (1994). *Designing Interactive Strategy: From Value Chain to Value Constellation*, Chichester: John Wiley & Sons.

Parolini, C. (1999). *The Value Net: A Tool for Competitive Strategy*, Chichester, Wiley.

Porter, M. E. (1980). *Competitive Strategy: Techniques for Analyzing Industries and Competitors*, Free Press.

Probert, D. (1997). *Make or Buy*, IEE Press.

Rappaport, A. (1986). *Creating Shareholder Value: The New Standard for Business Performance*, New York. The Free Press, A Division of Macmillan Publishers.

Riemann, (1987). Theory, strategy and entrepreneurship, in *The Competitive Challenge*, D. Teece, (ed.), Ballinger.

Scott, M. (1990). *Value Drivers: The Manager's Framework for Identifying the Drivers of Corporate Value Creation*, John Willy & Sons.

Stewart, G. B. (1990). The quest for value: the EVATM management guide. *Harper-Business*, New York.

Sutton, C. (1998). *Strategic Concepts*, London, MacMillan Business.

Waldron, D. (1999). Manufacturing strategy: what does it take to be world class, *ABAS Conference* July 12–14 Barcelona, Spain.

Warner A. and A. Hennel (2001). *Shareholder Value Explained*, Pearson Education.

INDEX

78–81, 83, 89, 100, 103–107, 111,
113–116, 121, 124, 129–134
value-based management, 11, 137
value chain, 4, 6, 11, 50–52, 75, 76, 79
value creation, 11, 13, 30, 130, 133
value delivery system, 49
value drivers, 6, 11, 45, 104
value enablers, 75
value net, 49
value-creating network, 47
variable, 17, 43, 44, 51, 53, 58, 69, 78
variance, 5
variant, 1
vision, 2, 103, 112
vulnerability, 99, 100

way of thinking, 2, 4
weakness, 44, 54, 107
wealth, 5, 23, 24, 27, 28, 31, 59,
107
weighted average cost of capital, 22, 26,
29, 44, 54, 57, 64, 104
working capital, 7, 26, 29, 31, 45, 53,
64, 68
world class, 8

yardstick, 25, 29
yielding, 14, 23, 33, 62, 63

zero defects, 78